Exploring Xinjiang

# Exploring Xinjiang

An American Family's Journey to the West

Patrick Wallace

Better Link Press

Copyright © 2010 Shanghai Press and Publishing Development Company

This book is edited and designed by the Editorial Committee of *Cultural China* series

Managing Directors: Wang Youbu, Xu Naiqing
Editorial Director: Wu Ying
Editor: Yang Xinci

Cover and Interior Design: Yuan Yinchang, Li Jing, Xia Wei

ISBN: 978-1-60220-310-5

Address any comments about *Exploring Xinjiang: An American Family's Journey to the West* to:

Better Link Press
99 Park Ave
New York, NY 10016
USA
or
Shanghai Press and Publishing Development Company
F 7 Donghu Road, Shanghai, China (200031)
Email: comments_betterlinkpress@hotmail.com

Printed in China by Shanghai Donnelley Printing Co. Ltd.

1  2  3  4  5  6  7  8  9  10

# Contents

Samuel, Emily, William, the author and John posing in front of the Flaming Mountains, near Turpan. It was more than 105°F that day. We all loved seeing the sights in Turpan, but with the young children and the intense heat, we had to get out.

# Introduction

I first visited Xinjiang in 2001. I had been teaching in northeast China for about a year and a half by then. Summer vacation came, and so I spent two weeks kicking around Beijing with the wife and kids. After we saw everything we wanted to see, we returned home. However, having more than a month of vacation left, I felt despondent. I had already seen Beijing several times before, and had only gone to Beijing this time because my family wanted to go there. Where I really wanted to go was Xinjiang, China's western most outpost—the heart of the ancient Silk Road.

Ever since I had gone to the Silk Road Exhibition in Nara, Japan in 1988, I had been enamored with places along the Silk Road. We lived in Osaka at the time, and had gone to Nara to see the temples and to feed the deer. While there, we stumbled on the exhibit hall and decided to enter. Inside, we were amazed by what we saw. From around the world, there were fabrics, spices, furniture, musical instruments, and artifacts. A cross between a museum and a Turkish bazaar, most of the displays were from Central Asia, a place I knew little about and had never even thought about before. The highlight of the exhibition was, mounted on a pedestal, an SUV that a Japanese adventurer had used to drive the length of the Silk Road. When I saw the mud caked on its windows and headlights, somehow I imagined myself driving that car, living that adventure, seeing those places. I was hooked. I just simple had to travel there one day.

So here I was, years later, pouting because it looked like I had missed my chance. After a week, my wife had had enough. She demanded that I leave at once. I had about $500 left over from my savings, so I got my cash, a camera, a few shirts, and a backpack, and took off one night. I spent several weeks backpacking through Xinjiang, and then took the long journey home. When I arrived, unwrapped all of my souvenirs and developed all of my photographs, my wife and children demanded that I take them. After some effort, I found a teaching position at a university in Xinjiang, and we ended up moving there. We stayed for two glorious years before moving on.

Some of what we learned, saw and experienced in western China can be found in the book you now have in your hands. Though I am by no means an expert in Xinjiang, our family is actually one of only a handful of western families that has ever lived there for any length of time, so this is Xinjiang through our eyes. Xinjiang, the way we understood it. Xinjiang, a place we once called home.

# 1 The Lay of the Land

In the far west of China, there is a large desert called the Taklamakan. Measuring 600 miles from east to west, and 260 miles from north to south, it is a large pit of gravel, sand, and salt flats. In ancient times, the desert had a vast lake in it which measured more than sixty miles wide. According to legend, on the shores of the lake there once

Typical vistas of desert and hills as seen from the train in Xinjiang.

lived a powerful civilization, with magnificent cities situated in vast oases of running streams and lush vegetation. If this civilization indeed existed, it has long since been buried by the sands, and the last muddy remnants of the lake dried up a long time ago. Today, mighty rivers run into the desert only to evaporate in the heat. Their riverbeds continue for miles, giving evidence of a land that once flowered and had trees. Here and there, small remnants of past cities and peoples are discovered near the lakebed. Like bits and pieces of a small jigsaw puzzle scattered in a large sandbox, these ruins are hints of a larger picture that has yet to be even partially reassembled or fully understood.

People say, perhaps apocryphally, that Taklamakan means, "You go in, but you don't come out." This is not a completely accurate description. Ancient caravan routes did run through the desert, so people did come out of it. However, many people also died there, and those mortals who survived it were counted as heroes.

The Buddhist monk Faxian (c.337–422), passed through the

Typical vistas of desert and hills as seen from the train in Xinjiang.

desert in his travels from Chang'an (modern-day Xi'an) to India to gather scriptures. He later described the desert as a place

> in which there are many evil demons and hot winds. Travelers who encounter them perish all to a man. There is not a bird to be seen in the air above, nor an animal on the ground below. Though you look all round most earnestly to find where you can cross, you know not where to make your choice, the only mark and indication being the dry bones of the dead left upon the sand.

Faxian recorded that it took seventeen days to pass through the desert between Dunhuang and Lop Nor, which is the quickest route. If so, he was traveling at a pace of about twenty-miles a day, which was exceedingly quick.

Marco Polo used this same route, but going the other direction:

> Now, such persons as propose to cross the Desert take a week's rest in this town (Lop Nor) to refresh themselves and their cattle; and then they make ready for the journey, taking with them a month's supply for man and beast. On quitting this city they enter the Desert. The length of this Desert is so great that 'tis said it would take a year and more to ride from one end of it to the other. And here, where its breadth is least, it takes a month to cross it. 'Tis all composed of hills and valleys

of sand, and not a thing to eat is to be found on it. But after riding for a day and a night you find fresh water, enough mayhap for some 50 or 100 persons with their beasts, but not for more. And all across the Desert you will find water in like manner, that is to say, in some 28 places altogether you will find good water, but in no great quantity; and in four places also you find brackish water. Beasts there are none; for there is nought for them to eat. But there is a marvelous thing related of this Desert, which is that when travelers are on the move by night, and one of them chances to lag behind or to fall asleep or the like, when he tries to gain his company again he will hear spirits talking, and will suppose them to be his comrades. Sometimes the spirits will call him by name; and thus shall a traveler ofttimes be led astray so that he never finds his party. And in this way many have perished. Sometimes the stray travelers will hear as it were the tramp and hum of a great cavalcade of people away from the real line of road, and taking this to be their own company they will follow the sound; and when day breaks they find that a cheat has been put on them and that they are in an ill plight. Even in the daytime one hears those spirits talking. And sometimes you shall hear the sound of a variety of musical instruments, and still more commonly the sound of drums. Hence in making this journey 'tis customary for travelers to keep close together. All the animals too have bells at their necks, so that they cannot easily get astray. And at sleeping-time a signal is put up to show the direction of the next march. So thus it is that the Desert is crossed.

Modern-day excursions using this same route typically take more than five days, but use four-wheel drives for most of the journey. Even in modern times, people die on such trips, the most famous case being the noted scientist Peng Jiamu, who disappeared in the desert in 1980 and has not been seen since.

In 1995, a highway was cut across a wide expanse of the desert, linking Minfeng with Korla. At about 325 miles in length, it allows travelers to cross the desert in ten hours. This presumes that the highway is not covered by drifting sand, there are no accidents, and there are no sandstorms. To travelers like Marco Polo, taking the highway must seem like cheating.

West and southwest of the Taklamakan Desert are the Pamirs and the Karakoram Ranges, which in reality form one long mountain range. This area is best thought of as the roof of the world. Mountains greater than 20,000 feet are common in this region, including one mountain on the Pakistani-Chinese border the goes by the name Qogir ("Qiaogeli Feng" in Chinese), and rises to a height of 28,251 feet. Most westerners call the mountain K2. Even the mountain valleys in this region are tall—most are more than 10,000 feet in altitude. The borders of India, Pakistan, Afghanistan, Tajikistan, and Kyrgyzstan run through this mountainous region. However, the only viable mountain passes through the area lead to Pakistan or Kyrgyzstan. In the farthest southwest of Xinjiang, there is a valley surrounded by the mountains on three sides, and by the Taklamakan Desert on the other. In the middle of this valley is Kashgar, which in ancient times was one of the most remote cities in the world, and which still feels like the end of the earth.

Bounding the south and southeast of the great desert are the Kunlun Mountains, which separate the desert from Tibet and Qinghai. With peaks more than 20,000 feet in height, these mountains are a place of myth and fancy. Huang Di, the Yellow Emperor and founder of the Chinese imperial line lived there in his

The Karakoram Highway as it traverses the Pamir Plateau, the roof of the world, at an elevation of more than 10,000 feet.

Jade Palace, and this was the domain of the Queen Mother of the West. Then and now, these mountains are largely uninhabited and uninhabitable, except by Taoist deities and Tibetan gods.

Bounding the northeast of the Taklamakan Desert is yet another desert, the Gobi. This desert stretches from the border of Gansu province up through Mongolia. Much of it is gravel and rock, though sand is also plentiful. Some of the desert grows enough vegetation to support sheep and cattle for part of the year.

North and northwest of the Taklamakan is the Tianshan Range. These mountains stretch from north of the desert town Hami, westward into Kazakhstan and Kyrgyzstan. East of Urumqi, these mountains are sometimes called Bogda Shan. While in

Tianchi, the "Heavenly Lake." Bogda Feng, at 17,864 feet, the highest peak in the eastern Tianshan Range, can be seen in the distance.

Kazakhstan and Kyrgyzstan the Tianshan Range can reach over 20,000 feet, within China the range is comparative foothills which reach no more than 15,000 feet in height. Despite their modest stature, many of these foothills have snow year around.

Still further north, past the Tianshan Range west of Urumqi, there is the Junggar Basin. In the middle of the basin, there is another desert called the Gurbantunggut. Some experts consider the Gurbantunggut to be part of the Gobi Desert, though in truth a low mountain range separates the two. The Junggar Basin forms a pyramid bounded by mountains. The mountains at the top of the pyramid are the Altai. This is a lush, alpine area full of trees and rivers. At the very tip of the pyramid is Friendship Peak (Youyi Feng). Its peak sits on the border between Russia, China, and Mongolia. At 14,300 feet, it is Mongolia's highest mountain. To the west of this pyramid is the country of Kazakhstan. Small oasis towns rim the Junggar Basin. One of them is Shihezi, which sits between the desert and the Tianshan Range.

West of Urumqi, the Tianshan Range forms a "Y," with one branch continuing west into Kazakhstan, and the other branch heading southwest into Kyrgyzstan. Nestled within the crook of this "Y" sits Ili. Yining is the largest city there. This area is famed as a rich farming valley. The lower branch of the Tianshan Range continues southwest, forming the northwest edge of the Taklamakan Desert, and finally joining with the Pamirs.

This, what is described above, is the Xinjiang Uyghur Autonomous Region of China.

# 2 The People of Xinjiang

From long ago, even before there was writing or paper, there were people living in Xinjiang—people whose history is as elusive and mysterious as the land itself. The oldest of these civilizations were no doubt made up of nomads, for they left few physical remains. However, they did leave their mark on the land, in the form of ancient petroglyphs scraped out on the rocky outcrops and caves surrounding the desert. Strange, two-headed people with triangular torsos and stick figures which look suspiciously like E.T. phoning home can be found, along with rock carvings of horsemen chasing wolves, and men hunting elk. Many of the petroglyphs—stick figures, really—of men and women have a strong sexual content. Are they connected with ancient fertility rituals? Or, are they just examples of prehistoric porn?

No one is sure who left these petroglyphs, or why. Since no two sets of petroglyphs look alike, these were made by different peoples at different times. Local experts averred that the rock carvings near the city in which we lived were made by Serbs. However, did the word "Serb" even have meaning when the carvings were made, many millennium ago? And, if they were Serbs that made the rock carvings, what were they doing in China? Indeed, some of the petroglyphs look a lot like those found in Europe or North Africa. However, many others look like nothing else found in this world.

There are hosts of other ancient anomalies that can be found in Xinjiang—a valley of large ballast stones near the Mongolian border, ancient statues reminiscent of the Celtic carvings found on the Emerald Isles, and stone circles not unlike those found in Northern Europe. These, along with the discovery of some ancient plaid cloth, have led some westerners to jubilantly proclaim that the ancient people of Xinjiang must have been Celtic, or even Scottish. Yet, though it might make a picturesque image, it is absurd to think of Xinjiang in terms of William Wallace or the Highland Games. Rather, these remains speak of a time in the ancient past when perhaps race, ethnicity, and countries did not mean the same as they do today, when small tribes of nomads surged in all directions, going back and forth like the tide, unsuccessfully looking for a place to call home.

The oldest culture in Xinjiang witnessed in written history was the Xiongnu. What little we know about this group comes from Chinese sources, as this nomadic group left little in the way of records themselves. Some petroglyphs particularly in Inner Mongolia, feature runic writing and appear to be from this group; however, the writing has not been translated. Were they Mongols? Turks? No one really knows. During the 18th century, some experts postulated that the Xiongnu were actually the same group as the Huns. However, the reasons given at the time seemed too highly speculative to be taken seriously. Ironically, many modern scholars have revisited this theory, and have found evidence that the Xiongnu and Huns were identical. Of course, this all begs the question, as we really have no clear idea who the Huns were, even to this day.

We do know that the Xiongnu were horsemen and terrific warriors. Essentially, China's Great Wall—the original Great Wall, and not the later Great Wall of the Ming dynasty—was built to keep out the Xiongnu. During the Han dynasty, many battles occurred between the Xiongnu and the Han Chinese. Though even in prehistory, there were Sinitic people living in Xinjiang, the first official Chinese military expeditions and garrisons in Xinjiang were in large part established to hold the Xiongnu in check. However, over the course of several centuries, the Xiongnu receded, and by the 5th century AD they ceased to be a threat. This is about the same time that the Huns became a thorn in the side of Europe.

A young Uyghur girl, posing in her Sunday best. Her mother thought that with her hat, her dress of Atlas silk, and her winning smile, tourists might want to pay to take pictures of her–and she was right. The mother is hiding in the doorway to the right.

Of course, there were other smaller groups of various obscure ethnicities which came and went in western China over the years. Many of these groups later intermarried with the Han Chinese and ceased to exist as separate tribes. Some maintained their separate identity. The most important group to maintain its separate identity were the Uyghurs, who at present make up more than 48% of the population of Xinjiang.

Originally, the Uyghurs were a Turkic group which had as its homeland central Mongolia. Through a series of complicated maneuvers, in 744 AD the Uyghurs conquered all of Mongolia, establishing their capital in Ordu Baliq, about 200 miles west of Ulan Bator. After gaining power over Mongolia, the Uyghurs allied themselves with the Tang Empire and fought against the Tubo (a Tibetan force) in the south, defeating them. The Uyghurs then turned against the Kyrgyz, another Turkic tribe north of them. The Uyghurs waged war against the Kyrgyz for nearly 100 years, more than holding their own against them, but never quite defeating them. Finally, due in large part because of internal divisions within the Uyghur camp, in 840 the Kyrgyz got the upper hand. They defeated the Uyghurs and kicked them out of Mongolia. Later, the Kyrgyz themselves were defeated and forced out of Mongolia by

Young Uyghur men, full of youthful exuberance. They saw the camera and demanded that I take their photo.

the Mongols, beginning a long trek which eventually led to what is modern-day Kyrgyzstan. A small minority of Kyrgyz live in Xinjiang today.

After their defeat, most Uyghurs began migrating westwards, intermarrying with the people there. One migration was to the area around Kashgar, in southwestern Xinjiang. The mixed-race people of this area later came to call themselves Karakhanids. The Karakhanids accepted Islam in the 11th century, giving Xinjiang the Islamic character it still has to this day. Other large contingents of Uyghurs came to Gansu province and to north and to central Xinjiang. They set up their own khanates under the auspices of the Emperor of the Tang dynasty. In the end, these khanates were smashed by Genghis Khan. Afterwards, the name "Uyghur" ceased to exist for nearly seven hundred years. The use of "Uyghur" to refer to the ethnic minority predominately living in Xinjiang today is a comparatively recent practice, dating from the 1920s and 30s.

The historical Uyghurs, like many of the nomads of ancient Mongolia, were warriors and horsemen, while modern Uyghurs are largely farmers who live a sedentary life, who use horses mostly for horse carts and plowing. Other ethnic groups in Xinjiang, such as the Kyrgyz, Kazakhs, and the Mongols have maintained a great deal of their customs and culture from of old. If we assume the same for the modern Uyghurs—that they have maintained much of the original culture—then they cannot be identical to the historical Uyghurs. Rather, they must be an amalgamation of different groups. One of these groups no doubt included the historical Uyghurs, but it is unclear to what degree the historical Uyghurs contributed to the makeup of the people currently living in Xinjiang. To reflect this, some scholars prefer to use different spellings for "Uyghur" distinguish between modern Uyghurs and the Uyghurs of history, and the Chinese sometimes call the historical Uyghurs "Huihu."

The historical Uyghurs have an honored place in history because of their writing system. Since they had their own alphabet and the Mongols did not, the Uyghurs effectively became the scribes and teachers of the Mongol Empire, producing government records and copies of Buddhist, Manichean and Christian scriptures. Their up-and-down script was later modified and became the basis for the Mongol alphabet still used in Mongolia today, and of the Manchu alphabet used by the imperial court of the Qing dynasty. You can still see the old Manchu script on placards in the Forbidden City. However, the Uyghurs adopted the Arabic alphabet when they converted to Islam, and today the main non-Mandarin writing system in use in Xinjiang is still Arabic, though the words being written are Uyghur or Kazakh. The modern Uyghurs are generally fairly short, and have dark skin. While most Uyghurs have dark brown hair, a few tend towards red or even blond highlights.

The second largest ethnic group in Xinjiang are the Hans, at about 40% of the population. As pointed out previously, the Han have had a long history in Xinjiang, certainly predating the Han dynasty. However, it was during the Han dynasty that the Chinese began a formal relationship with the area. Over the centuries, just as Chinese people migrated throughout Asia and the rest of the world, there was a gradual migration of Han into Xinjiang, and from long ago predominately Han cities existed by themselves or side-by-side with cities populated by other ethnic groups. An example of this was the ancient city of Jiaohe, which in the Tang dynasty existed as a predominately Han city very near Gaochang, a Uyghur city.

One of our dearest friends was a Han whose family had lived in Xinjiang for several hundred years. However, most of the Han we knew came to Xinjiang with the *Bingtuan*. The *Bingtuan* is the informal name of the Xinjiang Production and Construction Corps (*Xinjiang Shengchan Jianshe Bingtuan*). Beginning in the mid-1950s, groups of Han youth from cities were sent out to carve farms and towns out of areas of Xinjiang which were largely unsettled, especially in the north and central region of Xinjiang. During those turbulent times, most of the people who were with the *Bingtuan* came because they were ordered to. Having said that, many were happy to go west as they hoped to make new life for themselves, tilling the land or having jobs that they might not otherwise have had.

The next largest ethnic group in Xinjiang are the Kazakhs, at about 7% of the population. The Kazakhs are a mixed race people, half Mongol and half Turkic, and proudly so. Historically, they

Kazakh riders relaxing on a hill near Sayram Lake.

came about after the Mongol conquest of Central Asia when the Mongols intermarried with the local population. Linguistically, their language is close enough to Uyghur to be nearly intelligible to Uyghur speakers. Culturally, many of their traditions were borrowed from the Mongols. Like the Mongols, their hearts are warmed by the thought of yurts and horses. Most of the Kazakhs in China live in the north and central region, near the border with Kazakhstan and along the Tianshan Range.

A coppersmith.

After the Kazakh, there are the Hui (5%). Essentially, the Hui can be defined as Chinese Muslims who do not belong to other ethnic groups. Historically, the Hui are not really one ethnic group, but are made up of several Muslim ethnic groups that either came to China for trade, or were transported to China by the Mongols to serve in army outposts along the border of southeast China. Over the centuries, it is thought that many these groups had too low a population to be sustainable, and so began to intermarry with the Han, absorbing the Han culture. Apart from their religion, many—but by no means all—Hui are culturally and by appearance ethnically little different from the Han. However, even for those Hui who are nearly identical to the Han, their religion separates and defines them. How can one be Han, for example, and not eat pork, which is the staple meat for most Han? In honor of the fact that the Hui are a distinct people, since 1949 the Chinese government has recognized them as a separate ethnic group, something which the Hui have eagerly embraced. While many Hui live in Xinjiang, they are present throughout China, and

The entrance to the Great Bazaar (sometimes called the Sunday Market).

make up one of China's largest ethnic groups. Outside of Xinjiang, most of the many Muslims one sees in China are Hui. While comfortably living side by side with the Han, there is a movement among them to create their own, more culturally distinct, identity.

Apart from the Uyghurs, Hans, Kazakhs, and the Hui, there are at least ten other ethnic minority groups traditionally associated with Xinjiang. These are the Mongols, Kyrgyz, Xibe, Tajiks, Uzbeks, Manchus, Daur, Tatars, and Russians. These groups make up less than 1% of the population of Xinjiang each and, with the exception of the Mongols and the Kyrgyz, they number only in the tens of thousands, if that much. The Uyghurs, Kazakhs, Hui, Kyrgyz, Tajiks, and Uzbeks are primarily Muslim. Apart from having a common religion, this is a diverse group. For example, while the Uzbeks share a similar background to and are culturally very much like the Kazakhs, the Kyrgyz share a similar background to and are culturally very much like the Uyghurs, but have a distinct cultural twist which is not mirrored by any of the other groups. At the same time, though they are often lumped together with the Uzbeks, Kazakhs, Kyrgyz, and Uyghurs, the Tajiks are actually a Persian group with a completely different origin from the others. It is a remnant of the time when the Persian Empire stretched to the borders of China and India.

The Tatars historically were another Turkic group whose homeland was originally in Mongolia. In their case, however, they were completely assimilated into the Mongol Empire and still have a close identification with the Mongols even to this day. Because of this association, an alternate form of their name, "Tartar," is familiar

Kazakh shepherds herding their sheep on a road near Tianchi.

to westerners as an old synonym for "Mongolian." This occurred because the Tatars who were incorporated into the Mongol army formed a large segment of its western flank that faced Europe: the Mongol army that the Europeans met in battle was primarily made up of Tatar troops. After the Mongol Empire declined, the Tatars ended up stranded in various places throughout Eastern Europe, Russia, and Central Asia. There, they settled down and assimilated with the local people. Consequently, "Tatar" no longer refers to one ethnic group, but to an assortment of very small, distinct but historically related, ethnic groups scattered around Europe and Asia. I only met one Tatar in Xinjiang—a strikingly beautiful coed who looked like she was of some unknown northeast Asian ethnicity. She bore all the physical qualities of a northeast Asian, such as a Han, Korean, or a Japanese, with no trace of the Turkic or Eurasian characteristics so common in Central Asia. However, at the same time she looked somehow different, like a people all her own, not belonging to any of these groups.

The Daur are an ethnic group which descended from the ancient Khitans. Their ancient homeland was in what is now western Inner Mongolia and Northeast China, and they spoke a language related to Mongolian. After the Liao dynasty (907–1125 AD) fell, a remnant of the Khitan relocated to Xinjiang,

Yurts on a hillside. In the sky above, there is the faint smudge of a full moon, shining in the afternoon sun.

and are still there today. They have maintained their shamanistic religion along with Buddhism and many unique traditions, but tend to speak Mandarin Chinese.

The Manchus were originally from what is now Northeast China. They had a language linguistically related to Korean and Japanese, and were a people all their own. As they conquered the rest of China and formed the Qing dynasty, they became spread throughout China, though the largest concentration of Manchus is still in Northeast China. The Manchus in Xinjiang are mostly remnants of army detachments and official delegations sent out to Xinjiang during the Qing dynasty. Since the Manchus in China have nearly completely assimilated with the Han, there are only a handful that remain who are of pure blood and who can still speak the old language.

The Xibe are another group originally from Northeast China. They may be decedents of the Xianbei, a nomadic group which was powerful in the 2nd century AD. In the 17th century, they were incorporated into the Manchu army and were posted throughout China. The Xibe in Xinjiang live primarily in the Ili area, and are a remnant of an old Manchu battalion. While the Xibe elsewhere in China now use Mandarin as their language, the Xibe in Xinjiang have modified the Manchu language to incorporate elements of their original Xibe language, forming a version Manchu which is unique to their group. Culturally, they have much in common with the Manchu and the Han. The Xibe are animists, though some have adopted Buddhism or a form of shamanism.

Though there was once a large tribe of Mongols that lived in northern Xinjiang, the Junggars, they were destroying in the 18th century when they fought against the Qing dynasty. It is said in some written sources that a remnant of Junggars are still extant in Xinjiang, but everyone I talked to in Xinjiang assured me that this was not the case. Since I did not have a close Mongol confident, I have no idea if my sources were correct or were merely ill informed. Nevertheless, most of the Mongols in Xinjiang live around the edges of northern Xinjiang, along the borders of Kazakhstan and Mongolia. The Mongols were originally shamanistic. However, most have adopted Buddhism. Though they currently live on the periphery of Xinjiang, their culture in many ways informs the cultures of many of the other groups in Xinjiang and Central Asia. In particular, much of Xinjiang's cuisine—including the ubiquitous rice dish pulao (*zhua fan*)—ultimately has a Mongol origin. The horse and yurt culture of many of the Xinjiang ethnic groups was passed down to them by the Mongols.

Also living on the periphery of northern Xinjiang are a handful of Russians. Since the number of Russians in Xinjiang is quite small, but at the same time widely celebrated, they are often the subject of talk by the inhabitants of Xinjiang. All during the time I lived there, everyone I met thought I was Russian. It was a daily occurrence to hear someone in Chinese explain when I walked by, "He's Russian." At that point, someone would begin a knowing lecture about my "Russian" heritage and how I came to live in Xinjiang, or they would all begin to speculate as to my culture and habits.

I only met one Russian in all my time in Xinjiang. Once, when we were in Bole, we went to a hotel to find a room. There on the sofa in the lobby sat a plump, bald Caucasian man in dungarees, talking on his cell phone in very fluent Chinese. Were it not from the context or the language, one would guess by his clothes, physique, the expression on his face, and the way he held the phone, that he was a truck driver from Ohio. When I approached the hotel's front counter, the Chinese clerk stared at me, afraid and not knowing what to say. She looked at the man on the sofa, and then back at me. Finally, in hesitation she asked in Chinese, "Do you have an ID?" When I showed her my passport, a flood of relief swept over her face as she explained that I had to go to another hotel down the street because this hotel was only open to Chinese. The man on the sofa was Chinese and could stay at the hotel: I was not.

There are several other ethnic groups native to Xinjiang. However, confounding some people's misperceptions about Xinjiang, there are no ethnic groups distinct to Afghanistan, Pakistan, or India, which are also found in Xinjiang. That is to say, while one can find Tajiks and Uzbeks sprinkled throughout Central Asia, the archetypical Afghani ethnic group, the Pashtun, are not a group native to Xinjiang. Nor are the Punjabi, Sindhi, Gujarati, Hindi, or any of the other Indian ethnic groups. This is purely related to the geography of the land. On the map, China looks close to Afghanistan, Pakistan, and India, but the Pamir and Karakoram mountain ranges which separates China from these countries forms a nearly impenetrable barrier. This is not a place where very many people live or would ever want to live, and with the exception of Khunjerab Pass linking China and Pakistan, there are few if any viable routes through the area. While it is true that because of the Karakoram Highway through Khunjerab Pass, many Pakistanis now come to Xinjiang for business or to study, this highway was finished only in 1986. Before the highway was built, the Khunjerab Pass was not a very practical way to enter China. Indeed, it is not a very practical way to enter China even today.

# 3  The Journey There

It is difficult, if not impossible, to understand what it is like to live in Xinjiang without coming to grips with how isolated it is geographically. During the height of the Silk Road, when people traveled by camel, donkey, or on foot, even without taking into account weather and bandits, it could take months to travel from Khunjerab Pass to the capital, Chang'an (modern-day Xi'an). During the Yuan dynasty, Marco Polo spent several years trying to get from Kashgar to Kanbalik (Beijing). When I first came to Xinjiang, I met two Japanese in Kashgar who were near the end of a bicycle trek from Xi'an, and it had taken them three months. This in modern times, with good roads and little or no concern for bandits. However, even as late as the 1950s, there were no roads at all over much of this area. In western China, the Silk Road was never really a road in the sense that we might think of a road today. Rather, it was a route connecting points on a map, much like sea routes passing over the ocean to connect distant cities. Only here, instead of water there was an ocean of sand and seas of dry gravel. Travelers unfamiliar with the area frequently got lost in the desert, and consequently died. In the early part of the 19th century, there were several attempts to drive by car through or into Xinjiang. These were major expeditions requiring sometimes years of planning, as since there were no roads there were no gas stations either—the gas had to be brought in on donkey carts or camels, and then deposited at caches buried at pre-arranged locations to be picked up by the cars later.

Gradually, things have begun to change with the coming of the railway—the only transport which is really convenient to Xinjiang. Rail service was completed from Xi'an to Lanzhou, Gansu

province, in 1953. This was extended to Urumqi, Xinjiang, in 1962, to the border of Kazakhstan in 1990, and then finally to Kashgar in late 1999. While there is talk of extending the line into Pakistan, since the technical difficulties would appear to be even much greater than the just completed line from Qinghai to Tibet, I will believe it when I see it. In the old days, the express between Xi'an and Urumqi could take more than sixty hours. It had

A short stop on the train line somewhere in Inner Mongolia.

only a few stops, of no more than fifteen minutes each. Today, with faster trains and some upgrading of the line, that same trip has been whittled down to less than 50 hours. However, getting tickets on this train can be difficult if not impossible during the holidays, and it seems that the holidays are the only time anyone gets a chance to take such a long trip. During the holidays, most people end up taking the journey piecemeal, by catching one of the more plentiful trains from eastern China to Lanzhou, and then from Lanzhou to Urumqi.

My first journey to Xinjiang was by train.

In those days (and even today on most lines), there were four classes of tickets—soft seat, hard seat, soft sleeper, and hard sleeper. Soft seats, which have heavy padding, exist on some shorterhaul lines, but not generally on long-distance trains. Most of the carriages on long-distance trains are hard seat, which are benches with little or no padding. Since long-distance trains are generally night trains, this means that the majority of the passengers have to sit all night with the lights on. With hard seat, there are reserved or non-reserved tickets. Reserved tickets mean that you have your own seat for the duration of the ticket. Non-reserved tickets mean that you do not. Non-reserved tickets are sold at small stations that do not get a quota for reserved seats, and at larger stations when the reserved tickets run out. There seems to be no limit on the number of non-reserved hard seat tickets that can be sold on most lines, so during the peak seasons most of the people in a train car might be standing—and they dare not even think about trying to sit down. Even though their ticket cost the same as everyone else's, a person with a non-reserved seat is a de facto second-class citizen in the eyes of the other passengers, and—more often than not—the train attendants. Depending upon the mood of the train attendant, a non-reserved ticket holder may have no right to stow his luggage in the luggage rack, to lean on a seat, to steal a corner of a seat, to sit on a rubbish bin or his bags, or to sit or sleep on the floor. Essentially, the non-reserved ticket holder is to stand next to his bags for the night, and try to stay out of everyone else's way.

During the peak season, the atmosphere on a packed hardseat car might be happy and even festive during the early part of the night. And, why not? It is a holiday and everyone is going on a trip. However, by four in the morning, all of the non-reserved ticket holders are desperately trying to sleep while standing, without seriously leaning on anything or falling over onto anyone. When added to the bright lights, the stuffy air, and the one jerk who always wants to talk all night at the top of his lungs, it soon gets very testy, even hellish. My record standing on a train was seventeen hours. I do not believe that I am quite the same person I was before I got on that train, but that is a different story.

Soft sleeper tickets are strictly first class. There are four wellpadded berths to a compartment, and each compartment has a door that can be both closed and locked. It is a great way to travel, if you can afford it and if you can get a ticket. However, soft sleeper tickets can rival airline tickets in cost, and even the longest of the long-distance trains only have one or two soft sleeper cars, so tickets can be hard to get, though in fairness soft sleeper tickets are often the last to go before non-reserved hard seat tickets.

For long distance train travel in China then, hard sleeper becomes the only reasonable way to travel. There are generally six berths to a compartment—three stacked on each side with a common area in the middle. The level of padding for the berths is directly linked to the age of a train. On the oldest trains, the padding may be nothing more than a sheet and a thin layer of cotton batting, while on the newer trains the padding can be nearly as nice as a soft sleeper. There are no doors to the compartment, so taller people (like myself) end up sleeping with their feet in the narrow aisle at the end. With three levels, the topmost berth allows only about a foot and a half between the bed and the ceiling of the car. There is a ladder on the end to help climb up there, but it can be a tricky maneuver, so I often had to wedge my feet against window sills, the middle bunk, a stranger's shoulder, or anything else I could find in order to get up there. At night, the lights are turned off throughout the car, despite the protests of some of the passengers. For safety, dim footlights line the aisle, and an attendant sits at the end of the car keeping track of who is coming and going. During the day, the common area between berths is one big party. The bottom bunk becomes a long bench for everyone to sit on. With six people facing each other in a small space, everyone wants to talk—it makes no difference if they are all strangers. There is a small table at the end, near the window. When lunch comes, people take turns using the table to balance their cup noodles on. Under the table is a thermos, which the compartment residents take turns filling up at the samovar at the end of the car. People typically drink warm water or weak green tea. Many passengers carry a recycled jar with a warm water and handful of tealeaves or wolfberries in it. They will nurse on it all day. At one end of the car, there is a squatty toilet with a hole that opens up right on the tracks below. Needless to say, the toilets are always locked when the train comes to a station, as no one wants the train platforms to smell like an outhouse. There is usually a sink with mirrors as well. This serves as a common shower room on the morning a train reaches its destination.

My trip to Xinjiang began with a night train to Beijing. Since it was the summer holiday, getting a seat was impossible, so I stood all night to arrive at Beijing's Central Railway Station early the next morning. Train tickets out of Beijing can be hard to get, especially during the summer, so I immediately went and tried to buy a ticket west. The express to Urumqi was booked up into the foreseeable future, along with all tickets to Xi'an and Lanzhou, so I settled on a hard sleeper ticket to Datong, a city west of Beijing in Shanxi province, which left late that night. I then went sightseeing in Beijing at the handful of places I had yet to see there, and finally ended up asleep in the waiting lounge at Beijing's West Railway Station that afternoon.

The train to Datong was an old one without air conditioning, so I left the window open all night. The next morning, I woke up covered in soot. When I removed my baseball cap from the hat peg, it left a dark outline on the wall of the compartment.

In Datong, it was the same procedure—I bought tickets on the afternoon train to Hohhot, Inner Mongolia, and then went to see the sights. Though a coal-mining town, Datong is not without attractions, the most important of which is the Yungang Caves—grottoes dug out of a hill and then filled with Buddhist statues of great antiquity.

Datong does not usually warrant reserved seats on trains, so I stood most of five hours to Hohhot, Inner Mongolia, on another dusty old train. I arrived too late at night to get onward passage, so I had to check into a hotel. The next morning, sightseeing again, but there was nothing much to see except the museum, which had Greek and Roman relics dug up in the steppes nearby, and a fair collection of wooly mammoth and dinosaur skeletons. The night, I left for Lanzhou. Again, it was hard sleeper.

The trip to Lanzhou stretched to more than 37 hours. At first, the train was full of people, but at every stop, more people

The Yellow River, near Lanzhou.

got out. Few, if anyone got on the train. In one small town, I got out for a moment to stretch my legs. It seemed as though everyone on the train platform crowded around me wanting to talk. A man stepped forward with a big grin on his face and took my photo. He told me it was for the town newspaper. A foreigner stopping at their train station was front-page news. Nothing much happens in Inner Mongolia, I guess.

After many hours, we reached Baotou, Inner Mongolia. I had heard of some foreign teachers who lived out there, so I was curious as to what the city looked like. From the train station, it was hard to tell. There was nothing but low buildings of brown brick stretching off into a flat horizon punctuated by smokestacks. After five minutes, the train took off again. To the north were snowcapped mountains in the distance. Between the rails and the mountains were prairie, and miles upon miles of sunflower fields. To the south, nothing but plateau and low hills. The Yellow River or some tributary of it intertwined with the rails, sometimes passing to the left, sometimes to the right, and sometimes looping off into the distance as it poured its muddy water into the fields.

Sometime after Baotou, the drinking water on the train ran out. After a while, a food cart passed by, and I bought a Coke to quench my thirst. The train was nearly empty by then, so when the food cart reached the next compartment, the men playing cards there bought everything that was left on it. The vendor sat down with the men and played cards with them, opening new beers when the old ones were empty. By late afternoon, the floor was a carpet of sunflower-seed hulls, trash, and beer bottles. The wind coming through the open windows whipped the green curtains, making the

Typical vistas of desert and hills as seen from the train in Xinjiang.

train seem as dry and desolate as the scenery outside.

The next morning, the train reached Lanzhou. I bought a ticket for Turpan, Xinjiang, as soon as I arrived, but the train did not leave until around 10 p.m. that night, so I took off to see the sights. Lanzhou rests in a narrow valley between dry, yellow hills. Threading through the middle of the valley is the Yellow River. Though it is common wisdom that the Yellow River becomes muddy because of the silt from the loess plateau in Inner Mongolia and Shanxi province, even as upriver as Lanzhou the river is already the color and consistency of chocolate milk.

I took the cable car across the river to White Pagoda Park, and tried to find a place to rest. The park is on a hill overlooking the Yellow River, and is full of lounge chairs that you can rent to sit on and enjoy the view. Several times, I tried to sit down, but I was always waved off by a worker muttering, "Tai pang! Tai pang!" ("Too fat! Too fat!"), as though I would break the chair. Since I am used to people unfairly criticizing me because of my size, I thought nothing of their complaints, but was angry that they would not let me sit down. Finally, I found a sympathetic guy selling tea who would let me sit on one of his chairs. I drank my hot tea, and then laid back. A cool breeze blew across my body. Feeling comfortable, I nestled in to take a nap, when suddenly I heard a crack and found myself lying in the dirt and the broken remnants of the lounge chair. I really was too fat!

That night I returned to the train station. The waiting room looked as though it contained over 1,000 people, and it seemed as though everyone was waiting to get on my train. Many carried huge polyurethane bags bulging with who knows what. Some carried two or three bags at a time. Since even one bag was bigger than an average-sized man, often you could not really see much of a person carrying the bags. Indeed, it looked as though bags with feet were stumbling through the waiting room.

When we got the boarding call, an older gentleman looked at my hard sleeper ticket and told me to wait.

"Most of them don't have reserved seats," he said, "it's better to stand back while they board."

He was right. There was a sudden rush of bags, feet, and a mass of humanity to the boarding gate. Babies cried, people shouted, chairs were overturned and fists flew as over a thousand people tried to fit through one small door at once. Somewhere, I could hear the sound of glass breaking. After fifteen minutes of chaos and near rioting, there was silence as the room became empty. I walked peacefully through the boarding gate to the train and found my berth.

When light came the next morning, we were still in Gansu province. The train traveled for hours through the dry heat and the yellow landscape, through the Hexi Corridor, a desert valley dotted with small, green oases. Our companion for much of the trip was a narrow wall of packed dirt running in the distance parallel to the tracks. This narrow wall was part of the farthest reaches of the Great Wall. No first-time visitor to this region, Chinese or foreign, would believe that this decrepit line of dirt was the same Great Wall that ran as far east as Beijing, but it was. Somewhere before Dunhuang, the Great Wall petered out and we entered the Gobi Desert—a plain of hot gravel shimmering in the heat, with snowcapped mountains in the distance.

We traveled for hours without seeing any sign of human habitation. Night fell and the next day was more of the same.

Typical vistas of desert and hills as seen from the train in Xinjiang.

Finally, late in the afternoon, we reached Hami, the first major city inside Xinjiang. I got off the train and looked around, but could see no sign of a town anywhere. I shrugged my shoulders and got back on, disappointed.

The train continued on, with mountains to the north, and the vast expanse of the Taklamakan Desert to the south. Finally, at about 4 a.m., we pulled into the station near Turpan, and I got off. After nearly a week of travel and more than 2,500 miles, I had finally reached my destination, a place which is, apart from some small islands in the Pacific, one of the most remote habited places on Earth.

When I returned to northeast China after weeks of travel, my family insisted that I take them there. So, one evening a year later, my family and I stepped on an express train to Beijing, and left Jilin province, which up to then had been our home in China. Our group was made up of myself, my wife Debbie, my daughter Emily (12), and my three sons, John (11), Samuel (5), and William (1½).

I had gotten a job out west by going on the Internet and finding the addresses for every university and college in Xinjiang.

I sent them all letters explaining that I wanted to come out there and work, but only a handful replied. The best offer was from Shihezi University, located in the city of Shihezi, about 90 miles west of Urumqi, the capital and largest city in Xinjiang. I signed a letter of agreement, and sent them my information for processing.

The school I was teaching at in northeast China evicted us from our apartment in early July because my contract was up, and because the apartment had been sold to another school and was now needed for renovation. However, we were not expected at my new school in Xinjiang until late August. This left us with nearly two months with nowhere to live. We would have loved to spend the entire two months traveling in China, but after closing out things and paying for all of our household goods to be shipped to Xinjiang, we were strapped for money. A private cram school in Dehui, Jilin province, a small town between Changchun and Harbin, wanted a teacher for their summer program, so we went up there for three weeks.

I do not remember much about Dehui, except that it was hot and each of the lessons had more than eighty students, from four to twenty years old. Usually, the wife and kids participated or sat in on the lessons. We lived in a hotel for the duration, and every morning someone from the school would come to take us to breakfast, which was always boiled eggs, congee, shredded pigs ears, and pickles. Lunch was most often dumplings or some dish made from dog meat (the meat tasted just like turkey). From what we gathered, apart from some German guy who worked as an engineer at factory on the outskirts of town, we were the only foreigners who had come to Dehui in recent memory. Everywhere we went, we were treated like rock stars, and sometimes a riot almost resulted as people crowded around to see our blond-haired kids. With permission from the police, we set up an English Corner in the city square. An English Corner is usually a time where people can informally come and practice their English, hopefully with a foreigner. In Dehui, every night that we had an English Corner,

In the hard sleeper train carriage on our way to Xinjiang. Samuel tries to take a nap while William rides atop him.

more than 400 showed up. At each English Corner we conversed in English with a few lucky individuals, using bullhorns so that everyone else could listen in.

When it was time to leave, the teachers and the headmistress saw us off at the train station. Since the train originated in Harbin and Dehui was just a small, local station, we could not get reserved tickets. It was impossible to find a seat, so we had to stand and hope that someone would get off the train so that we could upgrade our tickets to either a sleeping berth or even a chair. Unfortunately, that never happened. We ended up in the dining car, continually ordering food and eating slowly, hoping that we would not get kicked out. When the dining car closed at about 2 a.m., the head cook went back to the employee sleeper and found an empty sleeping berth which he allowed the wife and kids to use. The five of them piled onto the narrow bed, which was not much more than a bench, and went to sleep, while I stood in a hallway between cars and tried not to fall over in exhaustion.

Beijing was a blur. Perhaps because of my exhaustion, I have no idea how long we stayed there or what we did. I do know that we could not get tickets to any destination west because all of the trains were full. Finally, we did the same trick that I had done a

Trying to escape the intense heat of Dunhuang. I am balancing William on my lap, while Samuel sits beside me. The patterned fabric behind me to the left is an example of Atlas cloth, which is the signature fabric of the Uyghurs.

year earlier—we bought tickets to Datong, and from there worked our way by train up to Hohhot, Inner Mongolia, and then to Lanzhou, Gansu province.

Overall, the kids enjoyed the trip. With six of us, we had all of the beds in the hard sleeper compartment to ourselves, which gave us a lot of privacy and also room to move around. We lived off cup noodles, dried nuts and fruit, and spicy beef jerky. When the kids were not swinging off the bunks, they played board games, read, or looked out the window. And when things got too boring, they could always break up the monotony by running down to the toilet or to get water, or even going on an expedition to the dining car to see if they had anything interesting on the menu.

In Lanzhou, we once again found it impossible to get train

Sunflower fields and mountains in Inner Mongolia.

tickets west, so we bought bus tickets for the most distant place west we could get to—Wuwei. Wuwei, an oasis town about 150 miles northwest of Lanzhou, is an old Chinese city with several ancient Buddhist temples. We spent the night there, and then caught a bus to Dunhuang, 450 miles further down the road.

This was just the first of many miserable bus rides in western China. At least on a train, you can get up and move around. However, these buses are usually filled to the gills—not only is every seat taken, but short wooden stools are placed in the aisles for yet more passengers. On such a bus, you are stuck in your seat with nowhere to fidget or move. The only air conditioning are the windows, but even though it is over 100°F outside, someone is always complaining about the dust coming in or that the breeze makes them too cold, so it is a fight to keep the windows open. Worse, you are at the mercy of the bus driver. He might stop for an unscheduled potty break and a meal for himself, but everyone else is limited to the regularly scheduled stops, no matter how many hours in-between. Adults can generally put up with this for a time, but it is rougher on the children—which makes it rougher on the adults as well. We always told ourselves that the next long-distance bus ride would be different, and, while some bus drivers were more considerate than others (and others were much worse), it was always really the same. In the end, we never took a bus any distance unless we absolutely had to.

Of the Dunhuang area, Marco Polo wrote,

The people are partly Christians and partly Idolaters, and all are subject to the Great Khan. The great General province to which all these three provinces belong is called Tangut. Over all the mountains of this province rhubarb is found in great abundance, and thither merchants come to buy it, and carry it thence all over the world. Travelers, however, dare not visit those mountains with any cattle but those of the country, for a certain plant grows there which is so poisonous that cattle which eat it lose their hoofs. The cattle of the country know it and eschew it. The people live by agriculture, and have not much trade. They are of a brown complexion. The whole of the province is healthy.

Today, Dunhuang is mostly known for the Mogao Grottoes, nearly 500 caves which have been festooned by Buddhist frescoes and statues. As the earliest of the caves dates back to around 366 AD, these represent some of the oldest Buddhist art in the world, and consequently it has been named a World Heritage site.

The caves were interesting. However, unlike the Longmen Grottoes in Luoyang or the Yungang Grottoes in Datong, one could not wander around freely in them. Rather, the entrance of each cave was completely sealed, except for a door which was locked. You had to be escorted by a guide with keys if you wanted to see anything. The caves you entered depended entirely upon the guide and his mood at the time. Our guide led us through about sixteen caves with little of interest in them, and then told us that for more money he would let us see some better caves. Since we had already paid a high entrance fee, we went away badly disappointed. We could not see much in the caves anyway, as none of the caves had lights. We had to depend upon small flashlights in order to make out anything. I guess if you had a good guide and remembered to bring your own flashlight, then it would probably be the trip of a lifetime. As it was, we found the nearby museum much more interesting.

We all enjoyed, the kids especially, going out to Mingsha, the so-called echoing sand mountain nearby. Mingsha is an expanse of sand dunes about 25 miles long, and 20 miles wide. I have heard that most of the dunes range from 180 to 500 feet in height. While I cannot vouch for seeing a 500-foot tall sand dune there, a minimum of 180 feet seems quite reasonable to me. These dunes were unimaginably huge—it was not at all like a walk at the beach.

Near the entrance to Mingsha, there is the famed Crescent Lake—a moon-shaped spring bubbling up amidst the dunes. We trudged through the sand to get there, feeling like we would die of dehydration and heat. When we arrived, we saw nothing more than a tiny pond and a drink stand. There was nothing much else there. However, from the pond, we could see people sledding down from the top of a nearby dune, and we decided that we had to give it a go. We tried walking up the dune to get to the sleds, but it was simply impossible. The dune must have been 300-feet tall, and we struggled just to climb just ten feet. Giving up, we walked back

Typical vistas of desert and hills as seen from the train in Xinjiang.

to the entrance. The wife was threatening divorce the whole way because she had had enough—there was just too much heat and sand. With that in mind, my wife, Samuel, and William stayed at a drink stand while the rest of us tried to walk to the other side of the dune where the sledding was taking place. We did not get far. Even though the path to the other side was a slope only about twenty feet high, we barely made it to the top, only to find that with every step our feet sunk a foot into the fine sand. We turned back, arriving at the entrance exhausted about forty minutes later. We had walked less than 300 feet into the desert. Desperate to get to the place where they were sledding, we now turned to Plan C— we rented camels.

Camels are fascinating beasts. When they are sitting on the ground, they seem no taller than your average footrest. You get on a seated camel by throwing your leg across the saddle, and then squatting down until your body is resting securely and snugly between the two humps. Then the camel gets up. First, he raises his back legs halfway up. You are now completely perpendicular, about six feet from the ground. Then before you have time to fall on your face in the sand, he raises his front feet halfway up, and you are pitched backwards, almost ready to fall off. Finally, his back legs go the rest of the way up, and then he stands straight on his front legs. You are now sitting more than eight feet off the ground. This beautiful ballet of camelidaen gymnastics takes less than a second to perform, during which time the average rider would suffer whiplash twice if he had time to think about it.

Apart from spitting at people they do not like or taking a bite now and then off your leg, camels seem well-balanced creatures, difficult to rile or upset. Unless, of course, there is a dog involved. While we were there, one hapless Chinese lady made the mistake of bringing her little ankle biter into the park area. The dog took off after a camel, yipping all the way. The camel made for the hills as fast as his legs could take him, dragging his poor handler behind him by the reins. Needless to say, the lady—and her dog—were evicted from the park.

I think that camels could walk through anything, but with their round footpads they seem especially suited to sand. They went up the first sand dune with no problem. From the top of the dune, we could see out over the tall waves of sand, stretching before us like there was no horizon. Within a few minutes, we had reached the place where they were sledding. Victoriously, we dismounted our camels. Before sledding however, we first had to walk up the wooden stairs to the top of a three-hundred foot slope of sand. We arrived at the top, exhausted and hot, and slid down the dune on a piece of plastic. It felt the same as snow sledding, except that we got sand into every nook and cranny of our bodies instead of snow. The only bad part about it was that it was over in just a few seconds, and then we had to climb the stairs back up to the top of the dune to do it again. After three or four tries, we were all exhausted.

On the way back to the entrance, we saw ominous darkness brewing up in the distance. Soon, we were engulfed in a sandstorm with a visibility of no more than ten feet. The wind wiped and tore at us, blowing off our hats, carrying away whatever we had taken with us, and making it nearly impossible to stay in our saddles. Hot grit filled our mouths and noses, and stung our eyes. The camels, on the other hand, continued on unperturbed as though nothing were amiss. When we finally got back, we discovered that we no longer had our camera. John and I tied bandanas over our mouths and noses, and went back into the sandstorm looking for it, but it was nowhere to be found. Even now, it—and all of our pictures from the trip—are probably still hiding in the sand waiting to be found by some archeologist a thousand years from now. No doubt, the photos will be held up as proof that the ancient inhabitants of the area were blond-haired Europeans after all, and that they rode camels instead of SUVs.

We all returned to the hotel, tired and complaining bitterly of the sand and heat, yet oddly happy that we had come to Dunhuang. The next day, we set out for Xinjiang.

# 4 Life in Shihezi

Ulan, our Kazakh *laowai*-wrangler, on the train from Urumqi to Shihezi.

We arrived in Urumqi and were met by Ulan, an assistant of the Shihezi University Foreign Affairs Office, who took us to spend the night at one of his relative's apartments.

During my teaching days, universities generally had their own Foreign Affairs Office (*Waishiban* or, more informally, *Waiban*, in Chinese). A foreign teacher would work directly for the Foreign Affairs Office, and the Foreign Affairs Office would also be responsible for the teacher's pay, living arrangements, safety, medical care, travel arrangements, and what not. Most Foreign Affairs Office had an assistant whose job was to keep the foreigners well fed and happy—a minder, or better yet, a *laowai*-wrangler. Ulan was to be our wrangler. Tall and fairly good-looking, as a Kazakh Ulan had that odd Eurasian look that many Central Asians have. If he wanted, he could pass as a member of just about any ethnic group whose people had dark skin. Most people, Chinese included, would find it very difficult to guess his ethnicity. In short, he was a Central Asian through and through.

That night, we ate *dapanji* out on the sidewalk in front of a local apartment which subbed as a restaurant. "*Dapanji*" means "big dish chicken". It is savory chicken served in a sauce with vegetables. It was the first time we had ever eaten *dapanji*. Ulan asked if we liked hot food, and I said yes, but in deference to my stomach and my children, would prefer something mild. He spoke to the waiter and the waiter nodded his head. Ulan turned back and said, "He promised to leave out many of the peppers. Don't worry: It will be mild."

A Uyghur kabob seller at the market in Shihezi. Most kabob sellers use makeshift braziers such as this. Often, they are mounted on the backs of bicycles so that they can be set up on busy street corners.

My wife and I both still agree that that *dapanji* was the spiciest food we had ever eaten, and we are veterans of Mexico, Thailand, and India. We know hot food, and that was hot—the kind of tasteless hot that in no way pleases the palette, but just induces intense pain. I have had *dapanji* many times since then, and it has never been near that spicy. I could not help but think that Ulan was trying to torture us.

Sometime later, when we had settled in Shihezi, I got to talking with Ulan and discovered that he had graduated from Jilin University and had helped at a language school there, I felt my memory stirred. I went to a drawer where I kept my collection of business cards, and sure enough, I found his. I had met him once, very briefly, several years before while coming out of my apartment. He was there with the manager of a language school, trying to find teachers willing to work part time. At the time, we had probably spoken for no more than forty-five seconds. Now, two thousand miles away and several years later he was sitting in my living room. As we talked, it turned out that unbeknownst to either of us we had a number of friends in common from our time in Jilin province. This was but a reminder of how fates intermingle and paths intertwine.

It was fall, and I was walking with my wife and William to go shopping near our house. There, next to the sidewalk, was a pile of leaves. I plopped William in the middle of it and took a quick snapshot. The photo could have been taken anywhere. However, if I had not told you, would you have been able to guess that it was taken in Xinjiang?

The next day after arriving in Urumqi, we took the train to Shihezi. Shihezi is a new city of about 500,000 people, carved out of the desert by the *Bingtuan* settlers in the late 1950s and early 1960s. Prior to groundbreaking in Shihezi, few people lived in the Shihezi area, and the land upon which Shihezi had been built was mostly a desert.

Though the *Bingtuan* is a kind of military unit, the vast majority of the people working in the *Bingtuan* system are strictly farmers, and Shihezi looked and felt just like any other Chinese farming community. The people who came to Shihezi with the *Bingtuan* were a tough bunch. Many of them, particularly with the university, were originally from Shanghai, causing the people of Shihezi to call Shihezi, "the Shanghai of the West." There was a story, which I cannot confirm, that one of the colleges which formed the basis of Shihezi University was originally located in Shanghai— the whole college, students and faculty, were transplanted to Shihezi in the 1950s in order to build a college there.

Rail transport to Urumqi was not completed until 1962, which meant that the first settlers had to travel most or all of the distance from the railhead in Lanzhou, over 1000 miles away, by truck over bumpy or non-existent roads. When they arrived in Shihezi, there were no hotels or houses to stay in, nowhere to buy

Some typical Chinese shops on campus at Shihezi University.

Streets on the campus of Shihezi University near the library and some administrative buildings. Such wide avenues and large open areas are typical of many universities in China.

food, and no provisions or tools except what they carried with them. There are few trees there, so the people lived in tents until they could build mud-brick houses. The desert ground, being mostly hard gravel, did not yield willingly to the plow, and in the beginning all of their crops—and thus their food supply—perished for a lack of water. Fortunately, the Manas River flows nearby, and there is a good supply of underground water from the runoff of snow from the Tianshan Range to the south. Over time, they were able to build a good irrigation system, and the desert blossomed.

Life in Shihezi was very comfortable for us. Our first apartment was a three-bedroom affair, with a small kitchen and toilet. Though very old and cramped, it was also across the way from the local outdoor market, and all of the nearby streets were lined with trees. Later, we moved into a huge new apartment on the campus of the medical school. It was nearly perfect for our

Much of the campus of Shihezi University was covered in fields of clover. Here are William and Samuel playing in such a field in front of our apartment building.

Since Shihezi University was surrounded by fences and walls, and had only a few gates, the people on campus would typically make their own gates so that they could more easily get in and out. This is the "gate" behind our apartment. Samuel and John have already gone out, while Emily poses.

needs, except that it was on the sixth floor and had no elevator. The view was nice, though.

Since we were north of the Tianshan Range, the north winds would get bottled up over us. This caused Shihezi to be comparatively cool in the summer, with temperatures usually in the 80°F. Since it had low humidity and usually a nice breeze, we seldom felt the need for air conditioning, which was good, since we did not have any. During the winter, the temperatures seldom got above freezing, and we often had snow.

The city did not have snowplows, so it, like most cities in China, relied on muscle to clear the roads and sidewalks of snow. Each business, office, and school was responsible for clearing the road in front of its premises. After a night of snow, the homeroom teachers at the university would have to wake up their students at first light, and they would go out and clear a predetermined section of road with brooms and shovels. To ensure that the students actually got out of bed and cleared snow, at the beginning of the school year each student had to post a bond of about $50 (for them, a small fortune). They would get this back at the end of the year, minus deductions for each time they slept in. One of my fondest memories of Xinjiang was waking up in the morning to the clank and scraping of shovels on the road. It would mean that the world was white outside. I loved walking in the snow and breathing the crisp winter air. Shihezi had no air pollution to speak of, so the snow stayed perfectly white until it melted in the spring. Right after the first freeze, the groundskeepers would water down the athletics' field near our apartment and turn it into an ice skating rink. I enjoyed watching the skaters on the rink.

Winter in Shihezi, as seen from our apartment windows.

Even though we lived in a remote area, with the exception of reading material in English, we could buy just about anything we wanted in Shihezi. New students and visitors were constantly amazed at the large electronics market in Shihezi.

"What? You think that we're just farmers living in the middle of nowhere? Of course we have computers here," Ulan would say.

However, apart from food, things in Shihezi were much generally much more expensive than elsewhere in China. This is because Xinjiang has no real manufacturing base: It mostly produces agricultural goods, handmade goods such as carpets and knives, and raw materials such as cotton and oil. While on the map, we were much closer to Kazakhstan and Pakistan than to Beijing, trade with these countries was negligible. Therefore, most things had to be brought over by train from Beijing, about 2,000 miles away.

We did most of our shopping at an outdoor market near our house and an indoor market a few blocks away. In these markets, everything imaginable would be sold off makeshift tables arranged in rows in a large commons. All kinds of fresh vegetables were in good supply throughout the year, and there were also many kinds of fruit available, especially watermelon and dried fruit such as raisins, apricots and dates. Spices were sold out of big burlap bags. Cloves, nutmeg, cumin, cassia, star anise, Sichuan peppercorns and red pepper were always in good supply. The meat section had no refrigeration of any kind. The meat was simply laid out on the tables or hung from hooks. You would tell the meat seller how

The apartment building across the way from our own apartment. This is the typical style of older apartments throughout China. It is based on an old Soviet design, except that it generally has enclosed balconies, while those in Russia do not.

much meat you wanted, and they would hack the appropriate amount of meat off using a large cleaver. Pork was plentiful, beef less so. Often, the beef was hung from a hook with the hoof and fur still attached to the lower leg, in order to prove to customers that it was not donkey. Selling donkey as beef was a common scam in some regions, though in truth, some people prefer donkey to beef. Chickens, usually freshly slaughtered, were easy to find. Some sellers would keep the chickens alive and let you choose which one you wanted to eat. They would kill it for you, plucking it and cleaning it if you liked, for no extra charge. Lamb was sold from a separate Muslim section off to the side. As it was nearly as cheap as the pork, and as they kept the area cleaner than the pork sellers did, more often than not we bought the lamb. There was a supermarket near the city center, but it was more expensive than the other markets and did not have anything we really needed or wanted, except for smoked turkey legs. That was one unexpected pleasure from living in Shihezi which made our Thanksgiving dinner possible every year.

As for food, the only thing we really missed was cheese. It was true that in some Muslim markets they sometimes had a kind of salted cheese, but it was dry and crumbly and had a slightly off taste, like it was going rancid. Certainly, it was not something one could use on pizza. Even if we wanted to use it, it was usually hard to find. Though we were assured that we could buy cheese in Urumqi, as hard as we looked we could never find it there. Finally, we decided to make our own cheese. Every morning, a Uyghur woman would come around our neighborhood with bicycle cart full of fresh, unpasteurized milk. Since there were no cartons to put the milk in, she would ladle it into thin plastic bags, and then weigh it to determine the price. Each bag could at best hold about a half gallon of milk.

Samuel with some of my homemade cheese, grating it for pizza. It was only barely able to melt. Nevertheless, it imparted a cheesy taste to the topping, which made it delightfully satisfactory for our use.

We began buying up to seven gallons of milk from her at a time. We would send the kids down the six flights of stairs from our apartment. They would buy the milk, and then lug it back up trying hard (sometimes unsuccessfully) not to spill the milk or break any of the bags as they went. I would then pour the milk into a ten-gallon pot and throw in some yoghurt to season it. After waiting, I would slowly add some heat and vinegar until the milk curdled. Then I would strain and press the curdles to make cheese. The process was decidedly hit or miss. Without a cooking thermometer or rennet, I could only guarantee a good cream cheese. A few times, we had some passable mozzarella, and once or twice I even succeeded in making something like cheddar. However, most of the time the product looked like some crude science experiment. Fortunately, we could nearly always use the cheese on pizza, even if it did not melt well, so we found our culinary cravings for western food satisfied.

Shihezi was the home of multiple Sichuan restaurants, and one of the best Uyghur restaurants in the world was located a short walk away from our house. This was the Big Mouth Restaurant. In Chinese thinking, to have a big mouth means that you are hungry and can eat a lot. As a place where the food was always wonderful, Big Mouth lived up to its name. Its specialties was pulao (*polo* in Uyghur, *zhuafan* in Mandarin; this was a kind of rice pilaf made with lamb and carrots), shish kebab (*yangrouchuanr* in Mandarin), *langman* (*banmian* in Mandarin; these are pulled noodles served

Our favorite eating establishment, a Kazakh restaurant specializing in horse sausage. Typical of many small family-owned restaurants and shops in China, it is a very small storefront on the ground floor of an apartment building.

in a thick sauce with lamb and vegetables), and naan (*nang* in Mandarin). However, all kinds of Chinese dishes could also be ordered there. Usually, this was where we ate out. Our other choice, which was a bit more expensive and therefore only for special occasions, was the *Siji Ping'an* (Four Seasons Safe and Secure) Restaurant. While the name on the sign did not at all give any hint as to what exactly the *Siji Ping'an* served, the picture on the sign and the inscription below said it all: There, below horses peacefully feeding in a pasture, the sign read (in Chinese), "Kazakh-style Horse Meat."

It was owned by one of Ulan's relatives, and for a while his mother cooked there. Upstairs, it was just a hole in the wall with six small, laminated tables and a fridge in the front full of beer and Coke. The chairs were nothing more than cheap stools. However, there was a stairway leading to the basement. There, in one big room was a carpet-covered platform supporting a large wooden table. This was their "Kazakh Room," where everyone ate communally while sitting on cushions on the floor. There was a small cubbyhole at the end of the room full of heat lamps and freshly made horse sausage being hung out to season.

Like most ethnic restaurants in Xinjiang, it served pulao, but with big chunks of fatty lamb and raisins, and on a platter large enough to feed four people. There was not much else on the menu, except for meat—roasted lamb and horse, and smoked horse sausage. The horse sausage would be sliced, boiled, and then served on a bed of flat noodles and sliced onion. Some of the leftover broth from the boiled sausage would be poured over the dish to keep the sausage from drying out and to cook the noodles. The sausage was absolutely wonderful—like beef, but more tender. We always savored every bit, fighting over the last piece of sausage and then the last bit of noodles. While we were sometimes unable to finish the pulao, as good as it was, we never once left any of the sausage, and often ordered seconds.

To this day, my children fondly remember eating there. There was something about that hole in the wall, a place that other people might have turned up their noses at, that touched us. The Kazakh Room was not that special, but it was furnished with care and with love. The food was good, but it was really just home cooking, made by people who knew they had something special and who wanted to share that little piece of specialness with the rest of the world. Unfortunately, few people even in Shihezi understood just how special it was, and the restaurant was always struggling financially. We are proud to say that we did our part to keep it going. Since leaving Xinjiang, we have tried horse sausage in other places, but it has never been nearly the same or nearly as good. This is one memory that cannot be replaced or replicated, no matter how much we try.

While the children enjoyed the food and certainly enjoyed living in Xinjiang, education and childcare was a constant concern. In northeast China, the older children had tried out the public schools with mixed success, and the younger two had gone to a kindergarten, which they seemed to enjoy. However, in Shihezi, none of this ever came together for them. The public schools did not know what to do with the older children, so they ended up relegated to the back of the

Norchayik, John, and Charles playing with kabobs at John's birthday party in a local Uyghur restaurant. The glasses contain a slightly salty, mare's milk tea.

classroom and ignored. The kindergarten we finally found for the younger ones was great. However, it was on the other side of town and had only one small bus which kept an irregular schedule. Often our kids missed the bus in the morning, or ended up standing outside for up to an hour in the snow. Then in the afternoon, it seemed that they were being dropped off at the end of the bus route, sometimes as late as 6:30 at night.

In the end, we gave up. My wife was teaching as well, but she was only teaching about sixteen hours a week, so we hired a Uyghur maid to cook and shop for us and to watch the little ones when my wife was at school. When she came home, she did what she could to home school the kids, but they suffered from a lack of books and other materials. Fortunately, the Internet provided a good lifeline, and we were able to find some material there. That, along with some learning programs bought at the local software store, was their main curriculum. To supplement the kids learning, we had university students come and tutor them in Chinese and math. This had only a limited effect as a learning tool, but helped provide the kids with friends.

Both my wife and daughter found a good friend in Mei, a Hui student from Ili. Towards the end of our stay, they were always chatting and hanging out together. Not only was she a friend, but also in many ways she proved indispensable to our life in Shihezi. She had good business sense and could often help us when we had problems getting something straightened out.

Another of our good friends was Charles. Charles belonged to a Han family from Hami. Unlike many of the Han in Xinjiang, his family was not from somewhere else in China—they had lived in Hami for as long as anyone could remember. As an English major, he had made a commitment at university to never speak Chinese. He tried to only speak in English, even with his friends. If he watched TV, it was an English DVD of CCTV 9 (the English news channel). He only read the English newspaper and English books. Here, in a small town in the far west of China, was a man living in

A feast under a grape arbor behind Norchayik's house near Shihezi. From left to right, Norchayik's sister, Debbie, Norchayik's mother, and Julia, a Han Chinese student from eastern China. The table is set with the typical sweet bread and fruit that would begin any Central Asian meal.

an all-English world—or at least as much of an English world as he could make it. Of course, his English was quite good. On the other hand, he often complained that his Chinese was suffering. Even though he was an English major, he still had to take an exam testing his grasp of Chinese characters before he could graduate, and this was a bigger problem for him than was his English.

On Sunday nights, Charles had on-the-air English lessons at the local radio station, where he played English songs, had discussions, and took phone calls from the listening audience. In time, both Emily and, to a lesser extent, John, became regular fixtures on the show. Emily became a local celebrity because of it. Fortunately, because she was only on the radio, the public did not know what she looked like, which allowed her some anonymity. However, her on-the-air e-mail address was usually chock full of letters from admirers. In the end, the show got a little too popular, and it was forced off the air due to internal politics at the station.

During that same time, I had my own brush with radio fame. For no discernable reason, correspondents with China Radio International came to interview me at my apartment and ask me about life in western China. I spoke with them for about an hour or so, and then forgot about it. Apparently, parts of the interview were broadcast around the world. The webpage for China Radio International still has me explaining in several different languages (but not English) that Shihezi was unbelievably and unexpectedly green. Here I am in German:

Charles on the air at the local radio station.

Ein Jahr ist es inzwischen her, seit Herr und Frau Wallace in die Oasenstadt Shihezi kamen, um an einer Universität als Lehrer zu arbeiten. Ein Jahr ist keine lange Zeit. Doch fühlen sich beide in der Stadt sehr wohl, wie Patrick Wallace sagt: "Es ist eine grüne Stadt. Überall gibt es Rasen und Bäume. In der Nacht breitet sich über der Stadt der Sternehimmel aus, und im Winter glänzt der weiße und saubere Schnee. Das Leben in Shihezi gefällt uns sehr."

Trying to sum our daily life in Xinjiang, two words come to mind: Peace and time. Generally, we led a very quiet, peaceful existence. The noise of traffic and airplanes was foreign to us, along with the hustle and bustle of the city. On a clear day, we could look out our window at the snow-capped Tianshan Range, and simply sit, marveling at the view. We also had time. Our teaching schedule was very light, and we had few if any commitments. With few distractions in such a small town, we had time for hobbies and messing around.

I remember in the spring, I used to go bicycling with the two oldest kids, Emily and John. We would try to ride on out to the mountains, and actually did get as far as the foothills. At the base of the foothills was the old city cemetery, the graves of which were gravel mounds with a narrow placard, sometimes made of wood, which served as the gravestone. The foothills themselves were covered in low shrubs, and we could see *doppa*-wearing shepherds and their sheep in the distance. We vowed to come back and climb up into the foothills in order to go camping under the snowy mountains, but we never did. On other occasions, we tried to ride north, out into the desert, but found it nearly impossible, as the *Bingtuan* farms with their irrigated fields ran for more miles than we could pedal.

With so much time on our hands, I began writing my great (and yet unfinished) novel, and spent quite a lot of time practicing the guitar. The kids got involved in this as well—especially John, who started his own great (and yet unfinished) novel. Later, for his birthday he got a blue acoustic guitar which had the single virtue of looking like it was electric. The guitar was cheap and difficult to play, yet could on occasion produce nice notes if the guitarist was careful, and lucky. After he got the guitar, he disappeared into his bedroom and we hardly saw him again.

We also spent a lot of time going to shops, looking for appropriate ethnic curios. Emily got a red Uyghur hope chest, traditionally festooned with gold sparkles and rhinestones. This went well with her Uyghur dancer's costume, with its scarf and colorful hat. The boys got Kazakh shirts—loose white pullovers with blue embroidery around the opening in the front. For years, they wore these as nightshirts every time they went to bed. Then there was the Muslim market on the far outskirts of town. It sold all of the typical ingredients needed for Uyghur and Kazakh food, and had a camel market next door. Once, I actually priced a camel on the nutty idea that I would go on a caravan across the desert. It was about 6000 RMB for a good camel which could actually go the distance. The problem was what to do with such a camel after you got done. As it turned out, camels, like cars, had a steep depreciation after sale. This was especially true of a camel which had actually been used for riding any distance over the desert. The best I could hope for after such a trip would be about 2000 RMB. With the food and other logistic necessities taken in mind, multiplied by two, as the older children would insist on going with me, such a trek was out of my reach financially, so I sadly gave up.

# 5 Teaching

Shihezi University, in both area and student population, is one of the largest universities in Xinjiang, and indeed, in China. The university encompasses over 430 acres. Maps and aerial photos show that more than a quarter of central Shihezi is university. Most of this land is covered with trees or clover, with school buildings, many quite modern, sprinkled throughout. The university has about 30,000 students, nearly all of whom are Han. Many are from areas outside Xinjiang, in particular Sichuan or Chengdu, but nearly every province in China is represented by the student population. As a comprehensive university, almost every possible subject is taught there, and it has a medical college, a dental college (with one of the most modern dental offices I have seen anywhere), and a large postgraduate program. While there is much for the university to be proud of, all of this, of course, is mitigated by the shadow cast by Xinjiang University, its hated rival in funds, students, and prestige, which finds its home in Urumqi, 90 miles to the east.

Apart from my wife, there was only one other foreign teacher at the university when we arrived, but neither we nor anyone else could really get along with him, so we tried to avoid him. For a short time, another foreign teacher taught at a private English school in town, but we never met him, and he soon left Shihezi. The nearest other foreigners lived in Urumqi, which might have been as far away as the moon, as far as we were concerned. Towards the end of our stay, a few Pakistani doctors came to teach at the Medical College. With them came about twenty Pakistani students. Sometimes the doctors would invite us to dinner, especially for example, during Eid (the feast at the end of Ramadan). We were never quite sure if they were sincerely wanting to become friends, or if it was part of their duty to invite non-believers over. At any rate, the food was wonderful and the company was not half bad.

The teaching itself was a delight. I mainly taught freshman "Oral" English (which means speaking, and not dental work), and freshman and sophomore writing. The freshmen had two weeks of mandatory army training at the beginning of the fall term, which meant that the bulk of my lessons began two week's late. I often saw the new army cadets standing at attention, marching, or getting yelled at by a drill sergeant as I walked through the campus. Since most of the cadets had never seen a foreigner before, and some would be my students, sometimes there would be a near riot when I walked by as they tried to get a glimpse of me. This would drive the drill sergeants bananas—they would bark out orders until they were hoarse, trying to get the students back to attention and to stop talking. I would just walk by as quickly as I could. After I got well past the students, I would sometimes look back at them, and invariably one of the girls would smile and wave at me. I would hear another bark and the girl would be at attention again, with an appropriately sour expression.

To help get the students more involved in Oral English, each of the regular classes of about sixty students was divided in half, so I had about thirty students at a time for two-hour lessons. In every lesson, there was always a student sitting on the front row who would demand that the whole lesson be "free conversation"— that is, no book or planned lesson, but just questions and answers. However, somehow, lessons involving "free conversation" always end up with the students not talking at all, with one student explaining, "We just want to hear you talk." Consequently, I always taught strictly according to a lesson plan, and tried to get all of the students involved, including the students on the back row who could not speak English well. Despite the vocal complaints of a few students, my student evaluations were always excellent, and I never had a problem with class attendance. The students were generally enthusiastic and happy to have a foreign teacher.

While the Oral English classes were a breeze to teach, the writing classes were quite a challenge. The rhetorical style of discourse in Chinese can be very different than what is usually found in English. While I am not an expert in the subject, at times it seems that Chinese essays are like a mystery which needs to be unraveled. The essay may seem meandering or pointless, but in the last sentence everything is tied together with a bow, leaving the reader with a final "Aha!" when he gets it. Sometimes, the point may never even be clearly stated, but merely hinted at. While this style of writing works well when it works, it can be very difficult to master. Even though they were writing in English, most of the students modeled their writing style after patterns found in Chinese discourse. While some people might not consider this a problem, a goal of the class was to help the students master the western style of discourse, so that they could better understand how it operated, and so that they could use it in their careers after graduation if, by any chance, they had to write something in English. To compound the problem, few if any of the students had experience writing even in Chinese. All of their study prior to university, and most of the study in university, consisted of rote memorization. If they had to write an essay in Chinese, more often than not, they simply copied or memorized it from somewhere else (often at the direction of their teachers). Consequently, as my Chinese colleagues often pointed out, many could not write a clear, thoughtful essay in Chinese, much less in English. As a result, most of their essays were a jumbled, incomprehensible mess, with little in the way of structure or style. In any language, their essays would be pointless and meandering. It took all my patience and ingenuity to teach the class, and there were usually few rewards for it.

Nevertheless, some students made it worth the while. In particular, there were students like Ping (not his real name). As a sophomore, he was in my wife's Oral English class and my writing class. Since I had more than sixty students in the writing class, it was very difficult for me to pick out at student, especially if the student did not come to class often or did sit near the front. Shortly into the fall term, I began to hear from my wife that one of her students, Ping, almost never came to class. She asked his classmates about him, and they expressed worry because not only was he considering dropping out of school, but they thought that he might be suicidal as well. As it turned out, he came from a very poor farming family in eastern China. His mother and father had saved up everything they had so that he could go to university, but now they were suffering hard times and were having trouble feeding themselves. At the same time, he was struggling in university, both with finances and with his studies. He was not the type to do well on tests that required rote memorization, so the other teachers had already written him off. At the same time, he felt incredible internal pressure to return home and work as a farmer or in a factory to feed his mother and father. Yet, to do so would be to give up any hope for his own future.

My wife asked me to watch for him, and I did, but I had trouble figuring out which one he was (I am simply awful when it comes to names and faces). Each week, I had my students write an essay, which I corrected and handed back to them. I saw nothing special in the essays that he wrote, but nothing particularly bad either. Then I gave them an assignment to write about a place they had visited, and something clicked. Instead of turning in one or two pages, as everyone always did, he turned in eight pages of passionate, beautifully written prose about a visit that he had made to a memorial to Zhou Enlai. The English was good. Very good. So good that it would have gotten marks in a university English class in the US. Not only that, but there were few if any spelling or grammar mistakes, yet the paper was obviously not plagiarized, as one would expect. This was his writing, from his heart.

I gave him a good grade on the essay and wrote him a kind note. From then on, every week he turned in at least six pages. Though there were sometimes some false starts or problems, generally his writing was very good. It just flowed. He had the gift.

A group picture of one of the adult education courses I taught for employees of the *Bingtuan*. The caption reads, "*Bingtuan* Second Public Official English Course Class Photo 26 December, 2002." Flanking me to the left are the Party Secretary of the English Department, the Head of the Foreign Affairs Office, and the Head of the English Department. Everyone else in the photo are students. To those with sharp eyes, yes, I am wearing winter People's Liberation Army boots. As it happens, the army store in China is the one place that has always carried sizes large enough to fit my feet.

Soon, he began approaching me outside of class, asking for my advice about writing, and about life. I heard through the grapevine that his class attendance was back up in his other courses, and that he had even joined a few of the school clubs and was now contributing to a school newspaper. There was no more talk of suicide or of dropping out. This was how I last saw him when we left Xinjiang.

I still have his email address in my address book. Sometimes I write him, but he never replies. I wonder how he is doing, and if he does not reply because life is not going well. I do not have a ready answer to this question. I only know that I was able to give him some encouragement and hope, to help bring out the jewel that was inside of him. This may not have been enough. On the other hand, if my wife and I had not been there to reach out to him, he would not have even had that much, as this was a person others had given up on.

Since I did not work directly for the English Department, most of my other classes were odds and ends dug up by the Foreign Affairs Office in order to please the other school departments or take care of other pressing needs. I taught postgraduate students so that they could satisfy the English requirements for their master's or doctorate's. I also taught classes for university professors so that they could pass various exams to further their careers or push them up the pay scale. Of course, one of my favorites classes was for civil servants. The government would sponsor specially selected civil servants to come and study at an intensive English program for a term. They stayed at a university-owned hotel at the edge of the campus, and had classes in a meeting room on the second floor. Most of their study would be for some kind of English test which they would have to take at the end of the term. My lessons served to help fulfill the speaking component of their program. In truth, their tests did not usually have a substantial speaking component, so my classes served as a kind of garnish rather than a main course. The students came from throughout Xinjiang and were full of all kinds of local knowledge and insights. They were all high-ranking managers in some state-owned enterprise or government department. Most were Han, though one high-ranking officer in the police was always ready at the first excuse to proclaim that he was Mongol and that everything good in Xinjiang originated in the Mongol culture. Teaching them was fun, because they were basically on vacation and the class gave them an excuse to goof off. At the end of each term, we would have a banquet at some restaurant. The food would always be wonderful, classic Chinese cuisine. However, few of the students would eat, as it was a time for karaoke and *baijiu*. *Baijiu* literally means "white liquor," but it has the smell, taste, and effect of rocket fuel. Such nights would end in a haze for all concerned.

Apart from my classes, I also took part in the yearly CCTV speech contests. CCTV refers to China Central Television, and it is the national TV network in China. Every year they have an English speech contest, with regional contests leading up to a final in Beijing, which is broadcast nationally. During my first year, I was one of the judges in the regional contest. That year Charles placed second behind a Xinjiang University student and did not get a chance to go to Beijing, even though I thought that he should have placed first.

A group picture of my freshman Oral English class, posing in front of the fountain in the university courtyard. That is William, pretending to be superman, sitting on my shoulder.

Partly for this reason, and partly because of some other shenanigans that happened during the contest, including strong interference from the other foreign teacher, who was not a judge and who was not supposed to be involved, I let it be known that I was not interested in serving as a judge again. The next year, the university asked me to be the coach. About fifteen students from Shihezi took part in the contest, and I worked with them both as a group and individually to get them prepared. Of course, some of the students did not want much help, while others were at my apartment nearly everyday. The one standout was Mei. Since she was already a friend of the family, she felt comfortable hanging around. She placed second that year: We were thwarted yet again by Xinjiang University. However, overall the university did much better that year than it had done in years of the past, so everyone was satisfied even though we were not able to send anyone to Beijing.

Partly as a result of this, I was asked to coach the school debate team, which consisted of Charles and a student from the medical college. After two weeks of intensive preparation, the two debaters went to Xi'an with Mr. Chen, the head of the English department, to take part in the contest. Unexpectedly, they placed within the top five as a team, and Charles came in third place as an individual debater. Again, no trip to Beijing, but everyone counted it as a great success.

# 6 Learning the Languages

Though at one time I was pretty good at Japanese, despite having several teachers, I have never been able to master Chinese. Grammatically, the two languages are completely different. Japanese uses particles, sorts of verbal markers to tell whether a noun is the subject or object. It also puts its highly conjugated verbs at the end of the sentence. On the other hand, Chinese has a typical subject-verb-object word order, and does not conjugate its verbs at all. Since basic Chinese grammar bears a strong resemblance to the grammar of English, but is in many ways simpler, my failure at Chinese comes down to a near inability to pronounce anything in Chinese correctly.

Each Chinese syllable can be pronounced with four separate tones—actually, five if you count the so-called neutral tone. Thus, in principle, each Chinese syllable has up to five different meanings depending upon the tone. The usual example that is given for this phenomenon is the syllable *ma*:

| 妈 | 麻 | 马 | 骂 | 吗 |
|---|---|---|---|---|
| *mā* (a high tone) | *má* (a rising tone) | *mǎ* (a dipping tone) | *mà* (a falling tone) | *ma* (a neutral tone) |
| mother | hemp | horse | scold | question mark |

When practicing, I can successfully mimic these tones in isolation. However, in a sentence, all of it comes out flat or just simply wrong. I can never get it right, no matter how hard I try. This may not seem much of a problem to you, but few Chinese people would ever tolerate someone referring to their mother as a horse, or to their horse as their mother, for that matter.

However, in truth the tones are the least of my problems. To my untrained and unsophisticated ears, for the first year I lived in China all I could hear of the Chinese language was *ar-ar-ar-ar-ar-ar*. Certainly, this was not what people were saying. Just as certainly, this was all I could hear. For this reason, my mastery of Chinese consists of a few short sentences and some scattered words, spoken incorrectly and only understood with great effort by the hearers.

My wife and children have not been likewise afflicted: They can understand and speak Chinese just fine. Apparently, they all came from the wife's side of the gene pool. Mind you, I can actually do surprisingly well at getting around in China, and somehow I often seem to understand much of the Chinese spoken to me, even though I often cannot explain how this could possibly be true, and even though I could not reply in coherent Chinese if my life depended upon it. However, this is not the same as being able to understand or speak the language. In that sense, I am totally lost. I might as well be on Mars.

With this in mind, I was delighted to come to Xinjiang. From my studies of Japanese, I knew that Japanese, Mongolian, and Turkic languages such as Uyghur and Kazakh are all Altaic languages, and so all belonged to the same language family. These languages all follow a subject-object-verb word order, and place the heavy work in the sentence on the verb and its myriad of conjugations. Since Japanese was easy for me, surely the languages of Xinjiang must be a piece of cake. However, as it turns out, there were a few hurdles to overcome in learning these languages.

The first hurdle: It seems that nearly everyone in Xinjiang speaks Chinese in daily life. Well, this is not exactly true. There are many members of the various ethnic groups in Xinjiang who grew up speaking their native language, and who might have a poor grasp (if any grasp at all) of Chinese. However, nearly anyone working at a government office, a state-owned enterprise (as most companies out there are), an educational institute, a hotel, or in any job in the travel industry will know Chinese and will use it on the job. Thus, while there are rural villages in Xinjiang where few people know Chinese, most of the people in Xinjiang that a foreigner is likely to meet—that *I* was likely to meet—would be speaking Chinese. It is true that many of these people would be bilingual. However, for them that means speaking Chinese at the office or in the marketplace, and speaking their native languages at home and with friends. This leaves little opportunity for a foreigner to actually practice any of these languages. Chinese is the national language of China, so I should have known. In Xinjiang, I was often just as much at a loss as in any other place in China, language-wise.

The second hurdle: though they are in the same language family, Mongolian and the Turkic languages are not *that* closely related to Japanese. I know of a Turkish lexicographer who swears that he has found over three thousand words in common between Japanese and Turkish. I suppose that this must be true. On the other hand, Uyghur and Kazakh are both closely related to Turkish. Since they are presumably more closely related to Japanese than Turkish is, because of their greater age and closer proximity to Japan, they must also have many more words in common with Japanese than Turkish does. Unfortunately, I could not find any examples of this phenomenon—I could not find a single word in Uyghur or Kazakh which was identical or even close to identical to one in Japanese.

It is true that many, many Uyghurs and Kazakhs in Xinjiang have studied Japanese. Further, they do seem to pick Japanese up quite quickly, and find a certain comforting kinship between the languages. It is also true that sometimes, just sometimes, I can hear a Uyghur or Kazakh speaking, and something in the intonation and the combination of sounds not only sounds a lot like Japanese, but is identifiable—I understand just that small scrap of language, just as sometimes when I am with Korean friends I can understand a little of what they are saying (Japanese is somewhat related to Korean). However, with Korean this occurs about 5% of the time, while with

Uyghur or Kazakh this occurs only about 0.5% of the time. Overall, the sounds of the languages are too different from the sounds of Japanese, and their grammars are infinitely more complex.

The first time I heard Uyghur was in Turpan. I was getting out of a cab that had a Uyghur driver, and as I handed him his fare, he said, "Rahmet." (It has a hard "h," kind of like the "ch" in "loch"). I looked at him quizzically, and then he explained—in Japanese, no less, since he could not speak English—that it meant, "Thank you." This was my first Uyghur lesson.

Later, when we moved to Xinjiang, we hired a Uyghur maid, Aliya, to teach us Uyghur cooking and the Uyghur language. However, it was not appropriate for a Muslim woman like her to teach me, so she tried to teach my wife instead. I do not know if my wife actually learned any of the language. My inclination is that she did not. It always seemed that she communicated with Aliya using telepathy more than anything else. They understood each other quite well, but I am not sure by what foul art or cunning madness this was accomplished.

After some searching, I found a book to help me learn Uyghur: *Travelling in Xinjiang: A Uyghur Conversation Guide for Tourists.* The book was organized logically enough. Since Uyghur uses the Arabic script, it began with a quick primer on the Arabic alphabet, and then went on to useful phrases, giving both the Arabic and a sort of pronunciation guide, which was a mishmash of symbols from the Roman alphabet, IPA symbols, and Pinyin (where "x" = /sh/, and "q" = /ch/):

1. Hi.　　　　　　　　　　　　ياخشىمۇسىز؟
   yahximusiz?
   How are you?　　　　　　　ئەھۋالىڭىز قانداق؟
   ǝhvalingiz kandak?

2. Thank you!　　　　　　　　رەھمەت سىزگە!
   rǝhmǝt sizgǝ!

Gradually, the phrases got more complex, finally becoming full dialogues with English and the pronunciation one page, and Arabic on the other:

| | |
|---|---|
| A. Are you from Kashgar?<br>B. I'd gone to Urumqi on business. | A. siz kəxkərlikmu?<br>B. hə'ə, ürümqigə tijarət ixi bilən kəlgənidim. |
| A. I'm from Canada. I'm going to sightsee in Kashgar. Let's get introduced!<br>B. Fine, I'm Hasan. Welcome to Kashgar. | A. mən kanadalik, kəxkərgə sayahətkə ketip barimən. tonux-up kalsak kandak?<br>B. bolidu, məning ismin həsən. kəxkərgə kəlginingizni karxi ali-mən. |

The book ends with a grammar key to the Uyghur language. It is all good stuff, and I am certain that someone somewhere somehow has learned Uyghur from it.

However, the book made my head swim. What exactly is the pronunciation of "ə"? Maybe I am simple minded, but from hearing Uyghurs speak, it seemed that what the text gave as "ə" represented several different sounds. That confused me. The mixing of equivalents in the Roman alphabet, IPA symbols, and Pinyin also confused me, because I always had to check back to the front of the book to see which symbol meant what pronunciation. Then, when I tried to simply read the text in Arabic, I found that the Arabic often did not seem to correspond to any of the pronunciation symbols. Further, the Arabic was often much too small to read anyways.

Of course, none of this was as disheartening as the grammar key. It turns out that in Uyghur the possessive of a noun is made by adding a suffix to the noun, instead of using a personal pronoun as one would do in English:

my child—*bal<u>am</u>*
our child—*bal<u>imiz</u>*
your child—*bal<u>ingiz</u>*
your (pl.) child—*bal<u>anglar</u>*
his/her/their child—*bal<u>isi</u>*

This seems easy enough, except that the suffixes change depending upon the sounds in the root word (this change is called vowel harmonization). While the ending remains the same, the part of the suffix linking the ending to the root changes as described below:

> If the final syllable of the noun has "a" or "e", then "i" joins the noun to its personal ending.
> If the final syllable of the noun has "o" or "u", then "u" joins the noun to its personal ending.
> If the final syllable of the noun has "ɵ" or "ü", then "ü" joins the noun to its personal ending.
> If an ending has a variety of forms, choose the vowel form that comes closest to the vowel in the noun. As for a consonant sound, choose an ending with voiced consonants if the noun has a voiced consonant sound and a voiceless consonant sound ending if the noun has a voiceless consonant sound.

When one considers that vowel harmonization is used throughout the Uyghur language, in both the noun case system and in verb conjugations, it is quite a formidable accomplishment to learn Uyghur from a book, and my hat is off to anyone who can do it.

I, however, was not up to this task, and I could not find a Uyghur tutor to help me. In both despair and in tandem with another crazy plot—to go to Kazakhstan and live as a shepherd, I decided to see if I could learn Kazakh (a close cousin to Uyghur) instead. Through a friend of a friend, we found Norchayik, a recent

Kazakh university graduate to help me in my quest.

Since I wanted to learn Kazakh like I learned Japanese, through both reading and speaking, I had him try to teach me to read Kazakh. This itself presented several hurdles. The Kazakhs in Xinjiang use the Arabic alphabet, just as the Uyghurs do. However, there appeared to be no textbooks or teaching materials for foreign learners of Kazakh using the Arabic alphabet. Norchayik decided to turn to teaching materials out of Kazakhstan for help. However, in Kazakhstan the Kazakhs no longer use Arabic to write their language—they use Cyrillic because they used to be a part of the Soviet Empire. There were some teaching materials for Kazakh in Cyrillic, but neither Norchayik nor I could read Cyrillic very well. Further, the way the Kazakh sounds were rendered in Cyrillic was different than the way they were rendered in Arabic, which caused confusion for the both of us. Considering the difficulty of using material from Kazakhstan, in the end we settled on a Kazakh primary school primer which was used in Kazakh-speaking schools in China to teach Kazakh children how to read their own language. It began with the ABCs in Arabic, showing how each letter was formed, and how the letters flowed together in cursive. All of this was using the Kazakh language.

The primer is a kind of monument to the Kazakh culture in China. The illustrations in it are all of Kazakh children, wearing traditional Kazakh dress. It begins with the children on their first day at school, gaily bringing flowers to their Kazakh teacher, and being shown to their classrooms before going outside to watch the ceremonial raising of China's national flag. The textbook continues by showing correct classroom and study behavior, children engaged in classroom chores and play, and correct dorm room behavior. This is followed by illustrations of the kind of landscapes, animals, and industries of northern Xinjiang. Just as in English textbooks, example words are used to help the children learn the alphabet ("'A' as in 'apple', 'b' as in 'banana'", etc.). However, in this textbook, these are sometimes unexpected. It is true that the first word is still "apple" (*alma* in Kazakh), but other example words include the Kazakh words for Howitzers, naan, saddles, and yurts.

I worked on the Arabic alphabet with Norchayik, and also tried to learn some Kazakh phrases and grammar. This was all slow going, as the Kazakh grammar is just as complex as Uyghur, and as I did not have much opportunity to practice between lessons.

Finally, Norchayik went to Kazakhstan on business. On this trip, he discovered that in Kazakhstan the situation was much the same as it was in China—while people may speak Kazakh there in their personal life, in business, government, and in the marketplace, Russian was more commonly used and more useful than Kazakh. This was somewhat of a shock to him, as he had assumed that he would be able to comfortably get around in Kazakhstan because most of the people there were Kazakh and because he even had distant relatives there. However, he was almost as lost in Kazakhstan without knowing Russian as I was in Xinjiang without knowing Chinese. For this reason, he decided that my quest to learn Kazakh was a waste of time. If I wanted to go to Kazakhstan, I should learn Russian instead.

Despite his misgivings, we continued on with the lessons for a while, until finally we were both too busy. Apart from the traditional Muslim greeting in Kazakh ("asalamu 'alaikum"), all of the Kazakh I learned has slipped behind a veil of forgetfulness, only to be brought out on those few occasions when I have a chance to speak with Norchayik. He might say something in Kazakh, and for a brief second I understand and perhaps can even converse. On those rare times, I am transported back to my living room in Xinjiang, with the big picture windows looking out at the Tianshan Range, and with a big pot of pulao being cooking over the stove by Aliya. The textures of our large Persian carpet and the sounds of the *dutar* and singing flood over me, and a place forgotten comes alive once again.

# 7 Urumqi, Tianchi and Turpan

On the map, Urumqi, the capital city of Xinjiang, appeared to be very close to Shihezi. In fact, they are worlds apart. While Shihezi is a quiet university and farming town, Urumqi is a bustling metropolis of over two million people. Like many large cities in China, it was in a constant state of urban renewal, with buildings going up and coming down, and roads being widened, torn up and rebuilt, which made it

Tianchi.

a mess to travel around in. We did not go there much, as there was nothing really that Urumqi had which we could not find in the local shops in Shihezi. We did hear of a store that sold imported cheese and food, but despite several treks traipsing about in the bitter cold and slipping on icy streets, we never found it.

Towards the end of our stay in Xinjiang, Urumqi got a KFC—the only truly western fast food restaurant at that time in Xinjiang. While there were a few other fast food restaurants in Xinjiang, these were all local concerns which could at times be quite dodgy. Usually, It was as though the owner had seen a fast food restaurant on a DVD or in a magazine, and had then set about trying to recreate it, without ever having actually visited a fast food restaurant or ever eaten fast food. For example, the buns on burgers might be sweat bread instead of real buns, and they might use shredded cabbage instead of lettuce. On several occasions, some sort of weird sauce made from paprika was used instead of ketchup. Our children insisted that we go to such places, perhaps in an attempt to replicate for them what might be considered a normal life. The wife and I suffered through it, eating burgers which claimed to be 100% beef, but tasting of pork and having the texture of rubber, and French fries which smelt of industrial oil. At the insistence of our kids, we went to the KFC in Urumqi a few times—it was always like Christmas to them. At the same time, we somehow felt that by the time Urumqi got its first western fast food joint, our life in Xinjiang was probably drawing to a close.

The one thing worth visiting in Urumqi was the museum. When you read *National Geographic* or see a special about Xinjiang on TV, there is nearly always a feature on the so-called Loulan Beauty and the Cherchen Man, two from among hundreds of mummies found in the deserts of Xinjiang. Many of these mummies and artifacts associated with them are on display at the museum. The mummies are every bit as interesting in person as they are in magazines or on TV. The Loulan Beauty, with her dark brown hair and smooth ebony skin, looks more like a sculpture

Tianchi

or statue than a person, which is perhaps why she is known as a "beauty." The Cherchen man, on the other hand, looks more mummy-esque. He has red hair, beard and moustache, and skin so light that the tattoos on his face are clearly visible. The clothes and possessions that came with the mummies are in many cases very well preserved. In particular, the red robes of the Cherchen Man look nearly wearable today.

Mongol and Kazakh yurts, some real, and some made of vinyl, at Tianchi.

There is no neat categorization for the artifacts. In one corner of the room, there are two-thousand-year-old mooncakes, now shriveled and petrified, giving evidence of the long-ago presence of the Chinese culture in Xinjiang. In another corner, there are sculptures and artifacts that show a clear Turkish or Eurasian influence. When I visited the tombs at Atsana (where some of these mummies are from), upon looking at a mummy in one tomb, a Japanese tourist turned and said to me in Japanese, "Well, with that pointed nose, he doesn't look Chinese at all!" However, in the very next tomb, there were two very Han-looking mummies, artwork on the wall which had a clear Han influence, and inscriptions in Chinese characters, to boot. The same phenomenon exists at the museum in Urumqi: The museum presents a multiethnic past, with an ebb and flow of many civilizations over the centuries. Those looking to fit Xinjiang's history into a simple narrative ultimately miss the mark. There have always been Chinese people in Xinjiang. There were other people there, as well.

Traveling west of Urumqi, there is a large wind farm made up of some two hundred propeller-driven turbines about 150 feet in height. Taking the road north from there, past pine trees and alpine scenery, cable cars and yurts, sheep and horses, and lots of buses, you reach Tianchi, the so-called Heavenly Lake. The lake itself

A goat grazing on the rocky shore of Tianchi.

is spectacular. Hidden in a cut between mountains with snowy peaks in the distance, the lake sits in all of its blue wonder. It is no surprise that it is one of the most visited places in Xinjiang, and that it was named a World Heritage Site by UNESCO in 1990.

At the same time, I hated it. There were just too many tourists, and too many tourist shops and restaurants. In many ways, it was like visiting Yellowstone during the peak season, but with a lot more people. However, if you hike back far enough away from the parking lot, down where you can no longer hear the loud hum of the speedboats which whip puking tourists around the lake, there is also real beauty and peace there. When I went to Tianchi, Kazakh horsemen kept riding up to me and asking if I wanted to ride out to the snowy mountains in the distance. However, like most people traveling to Tianchi, I had to catch a bus back to Urumqi, so I took a rain check and told them I would go riding next time. But I could never bring myself to go back.

Now, looking over my photos of Tianchi, I regret this, as the photos make the place look stunningly beautiful. Perhaps in my annoyance at finding myself among so many other people, I missed what was special about Tianchi, and could not see the beauty that was right in front of me, that my camera captured, but I could not comprehend. I should have ridden with the horsemen up to the snowy mountains. That would have been quite a trip.

Taking the road south after the wind farm, you wind through the mountains until you reach the desert and Turpan. With a population of about 500,000 people, mostly Uyghurs, Turpan has been settled for well over 2,000 years. An oasis town, it is famous for promenades and outdoor cafes, shaded by grape arbors. This is

The entrance to a grape arbor covered shopping arcade in Turpan. Note the typical Uyghur decorative architecture on the gate.

an excellent place to see Uyghur dancing and hear Uyghur music. It is also the site of the Flaming Mountains, which is mentioned prominently in the ancient and beloved Chinese novel, *The Journey to the West*. In this tale, the Monkey King, Pigsy (his half-man, half-pig friend), and the monk Xuanzang are on a quest to India to find some sacred scriptures. On their way there, they endure many ordeals, one of which is the Flaming Mountains. Unbeknownst to the travelers, the Monkey King himself inadvertently formed the mountains some five hundred years prior to their arrival. It seems that the Monkey King was wrecking havoc in the heavens, and the Jade Emperor put him into a furnace to be refined. When the Monkey King was finally released from the furnace, he kicked the furnace over in anger, causing its embers to fall to the earth and form the Flaming Mountains.

This is how the mountains were described in *The Journey to the West*, by an old man in Gaochang, the nearby walled city:

Xuanzang rose to his feet to thank the old man and ask, "Could you tell me, sir, why it has turned so hot again although it is autumn now?"

"These are the Fiery Mountains," the old man replied. "We don't have springs or autumns here. It's hot all the year round."

"Where are the mountains?" Xuanzang asked. "Do they block the way to the West?"

"It's impossible to get to the West," the old man replied. "The mountains are about twenty miles from here. You have to cross them to get to the West, but they're over 250 miles of flame. Not a blade of grass can grow anywhere around. Even if you had a skull of bronze and a body of iron you would melt trying to cross them."

This answer made Xuanzang turn pale with horror; he dared not to ask any more questions.

There is much truth to this, except that the mountains are not as large as the old man said—they are only about 60 miles long and six miles wide. Made of weathered red sandstone, the mountains form a high ridge jutting nearly straight up out of the desert floor. When the sun is low in the sky, its rays turn the mountains bright red, making them look like mountain of fire. As most Chinese have grown up on stories of the Monkey King, this is one of the most popular tourist spot in the Turpan region, and some people make a pilgrimage to Xinjiang just to see this sight. However, people not so familiar with the Monkey King will be less impressed.

Apart from the many sites of historical and cultural interest, Turpan has two main distinctives:

Turpan means "lowest place" in Uyghur, and indeed, the area has some of the lowest elevations on earth. This is particularly true of Aydingkol Lake, about twenty miles south of the Turpan city center. At nearly 500 feet below sea level, it is the second lowest lake in the world next to the Dead Sea. Like the Dead Sea, because it has no outlet it is a salt lake. This is not a good place to visit, because most of the year it is just a big, salty mud puddle.

As a second distinctive, Turpan is the hottest place in China. The highest temperature recorded there was 121°F, and the times we visited there the thermometer at the hotel routinely registered around 113°F. Desert heat is often bearable because the lack of humidity cools you down. Not here. Turpan is an oven. Having said that, it was also one of our favorite places in the world, and we were all happy to go there, though the heat always caused us to cut our trips short.

A grape arbor covered shopping arcade in Turpan. It looks cool under the shade–and it was, a little.

One fascinating aspect of Turpan are the karez. The Turpan area has little in the way of fresh water, but the Tianshan Range to the north has enough snow to provide more than enough water for the needs of the people living there. However, the intense heat causes water in irrigation ditches to quickly evaporate, making farming impossible. To solve this problem, karez (irrigation tunnels) were dug by hand about twenty to thirty feet below the desert surface. These carry water as far as 40 miles from the Tianshan Range to the farms out in the desert. By far the largest produce of these farms are grapes. In ancient times, this was a major wine-producing area. However, with the advent of Islam, most of the vintners turned to producing raisins, though some wine is still made. Almonds, apricots, and watermelon are also grown in abundance.

Each karez is linked to the surface by wells which are spaced several hundred yards apart. These can often be seen sprouting up out of the desert floor when you are driving around. Though this technology was originally developed by the Persians, the karez system near Turpan is one of the largest and oldest in the world. No one knows for certain when it was built, but guesses range from 2,000 to 3,000 years ago. The total length of karez which are currently being used exceeds 3,000 kilometers. The last time we were in Turpan, they had finally built a karez museum, where the whole system could be explained and where you could actually go down into a karez and walk down a length of the tunnel. It was a great place to visit, and not just because the museum had air conditioning and the karez was naturally cool.

The Emin Khoja Mosque and Minaret.

The two tourist sites we enjoyed most in Turpan were the Emin Khoja Mosque and Minaret, and the ancient city of Gaochang.

The Emin Khoja Mosque and Minaret was built in 1777–1788 by Suleyman Khoja (sometimes spelled as "Hoja") in honor of his father, Emin Khoja. "Khoja," a title meaning "master," was not originally a family name, but was applied to all of the decedents of the Sufi sage, Ahmad Kasani (1461–1542), who was from what is now Uzbekistan. Kasani sent his progeny out to be missionaries and teachers throughout Central Asia. Though these men were not Uyghur, when they came to Xinjiang they set themselves up in positions of authority over the people there. In the beginning, it seems that the local residents publicly recognized the Khojas' authority, but may have privately ignored them. This presented a powerful incentive on the Khojas to do whatever they could to build their prestige among the common people.

In the seventeenth and eighteenth centuries, there was a conflict between the Junggars, a Mongol group which was then extant in northern Xinjiang, and the Qing dynasty. In effect, the

The entrance to the Emin Khoja Mosque in Turpan is a good example of classical Afghani style architecture.

Inside the main hall of the Emin Khoja Mosque, looking towards the altar where the Koran would be kept.

Junggar leaders were trying to reunite the Mongol tribes and resurrect the glory of the Mongolian Empire. To help fight against the Junggars, the Qing dynasty made a deal with Emin Khoja: The Qing dynasty would recognize Emin Khoja's authority over the Turpan area (as a liege of the Emperor) and buttress his rule there. In return, Emin Khoja would swear allegiance to the Emperor and raise an army to protect the Emperor's flanks. In 1755, the Emperor defeated the Junggars and captured their khan in a battle at Yining. Emin Khoja profited handsomely, both in prestige and financially, from this endeavor, receiving 7,000 pieces of silver from the Emperor.

In one legend, Emin Khoja began using the silver to build a palace for himself. However, when the Emperor in Beijing heard this, he suspected treachery and threatened to remove Emin Khoja and his son from power. To placate the Emperor, a minaret was quickly added to the building, and messengers were sent back to assure him that it was not a palace, but was a mosque. Thus placated, the Emperor let the construction proceed, and so the Emin Khoja Mosque and Minaret was completed.

On the roof on Emin Khoja Mosque, looking out over nearby vineyards. The Turpan area historically specialized in viniculture. However, after Islam came to the area, most of the farmers stopped producing grapes for wine, and began making raisins instead. The small brick buildings in the background of the photo are drying huts for the grapes. Since the sun is too intense for making raisins, the grapes are placed still on the vine in these huts, where the wind quickly desiccates them.

The Mosque and Minaret is one of the most impressive pieces of architecture in China. Made of brick, with clean, unadorned lines, it is reminiscent of the mosques in Afghanistan, rather than the more typically ornate style preferred by the Uyghurs. Inside, in addition to some smaller rooms in the back, the Mosque has one central room for prayer that can hold about 1,000 people. Its ceiling is supported by beams of poplar and is surmounted by a large dome. All of the interior light is provided by skylights cut into the ceiling or by windows. Stairs lead to the roof, from which you can get a good view of the vineyards and the brick drying-houses for the raisins. The Minaret, at 116 feet in height, is the tallest in China. The inner core of the Minaret is nothing but a spiral staircase leading to the platform at the top. No beams were used in its construction. To help preserve the Minaret, it has been closed to the public since 1989. The Mosque itself, as a national treasure, is not used for prayer anymore except on some festival days.

While the Emin Khoja Mosque and Minaret is an architectural treasure, Gaochang is literally just a pile of ruins. It is not as old

The ruins at Gaochang.

The remains of the dagoba at Gaochang.

The ruins at Gaochang.

The ruins of the dagoba and a sub-temple at Gaochang.

The ruins at Gaochang.

or as well preserved as the nearby ruins of Jiaohe, but its history is much more fascinating to me. The city traces back to the Western Han dynasty, in the late second century BC, when Chinese armies marched west to wage war against the Xiongnu. During the Eastern Han dynasty, the Chinese garrison moved from Jiaohe to Gaochang, and in 327 AD, Gaochang was established as a county. In the centuries that followed, many wars were fought in the Gaochang area as various dynasties and tribes tried to control the area. Finally, in the mid ninth century, the Uyghurs took control of the city.

This occurred after the Uyghurs were kicked out of Mongolia by the Kyrgyz. The Uyghurs went west and those who settled in Gaochang turned to the Tang dynasty. In return for giving their allegiance to the emperor and fighting against the now resurgent Tubo, the Uyghurs were given Gaochang and were incorporated into the Tang empire. Unlike the Uyghurs who settled in the Kashgar region and adopted Islam, the Uyghurs in Gaochang were primarily Buddhist. Gaochang remained the Uyghur capital until 1275, when a Mongol army of 120,000 men besieged and destroyed it. Over time, people drifted back to the city and began rebuilding it. However, in 1383, the ruler of Gaochang decided to wage war against the nearby town of Turpan. However, he bit off more than he could chew, and what was left of Gaochang was

Since the ruins of Gaochang are so large, the traditional Uyghur form of travel, donkey carts, are used to transport people. The two Uyghur girls in the foreground are wearing clothes made of Atlas silk.

destroyed. The city was never rebuilt.

The immense ruins of Gaochang form a mile-wide square. Large sections of the twenty-foot high city walls are still intact, and the foundations of most of the buildings are still visible. A Buddhist temple complex in the southwest corner of the city is easily identifiable. Despite the intense heat, it is a fascinating place to spend the day. There are all kinds of nooks and crannies to explore. Though we would not let the children take them home, the ground was littered with pottery shard and archeological

trinkets, which the kids spent hours looking for and examining. The children enjoyed climbing to the tops of the walls to get a view of they city and the surrounding countryside. Their fantasies ran riot as they speculated on what must have been, and on how the people must have lived.

Remains of one of the city gates of Gaochang.

# 8 Our First Yurt

We had been to a yurt before.

It was for a party out in the desert. Ulan called and asked if we wanted to go, so Emily, John and I piled into a jeep and took off driving into the darkness. We pulled off the highway onto a gravel road and drove into a complex of yurts gathered surrounded by knee-high white picket fences. The yurts themselves were completely

Our dwelling at Sayram Lake.

white, and were made of canvas laminated with vinyl. In the headlights, they shone like giant igloos against the night, almost blinding us. The effect was sterile and pristine, like something you would see in a hospital. Indeed, I once did see a yurt like one of those on the grounds of a hospital in Shanghai. I have no idea what it was doing there, but with the yurt seemed to fit, as it was as clean and white as the tile walls of a hospital corridor, with not a speck of dirt marring its shiny surface.

Even in the desert darkness, one could tell that these yurts were not anything that a person would ever or could ever actually live in. More than forty feet wide and standing on concrete foundations, they were more like great pavilions or halls than tents. Each had a solid wooden door mounted on a frame, with a heavy lock keeping out intruders.

The jeep stopped at the only yurt with light, and as we opened the door, we could hear disco music blaring in the background, disturbing the calm of the night. We entered to find a room full of Pakistani medical students and a handful of Chinese sitting on the carpeted floor, finishing off some kebab and beer while they watched two other students dance together in front of a big screen TV set playing the latest music videos from India and Turkey. (The Pakistanis preferred these, because Pakistani music videos seldom had women singers or dancers.) The two students dancing together were, naturally, men. Mind you, the men dancing together did not seem the least bit effeminate; rather, it was a pure show of machismo. One man would do some dance moves, wagging his behind and moving his hands like a hula dancer, while the other man watched quietly, rocking on his heels to the beat of techno-pop. Then it became his turn to show off. It was like two peacocks strutting their stuff to one another, as if to say, "Can you top this?" Impressive, but to what effect? The handful of females in the yurt sat discretely talking together, apparently oblivious to the show.

We sat down to join the party, but we had arrived late so most of the food was gone. There had been a big pan of pulao, more than three feet across, but there was little left of the rice except some greasy black suet from the bottom of the pan. We were able to rustle up some kebab, but it was now cold, and the lamb fat had congealed into little white balls that looked like frosting, but tasted like chalky paste.

Of course, there was still plenty of Wusu Beer, so a few of the men got totally wasted and began to make vocal threats that they were going to kick each other's butts. Finally, they settled on Ulan. Two men grabbed him and held him in the air, while another man kicked him in the butt with his boots. The men were laughing so hard that they finally dropped Ulan on the floor, while Ulan tried to round up a few other men to get revenge on his attackers. It was all in good fun.

Meanwhile, one of the drunken Chinese students kept hitting on Emily, who could not have been more than twelve at the time.

Sayram Lake.

"Come on! Dance with me! Do you wanna dance? Do you wanna dance?" he kept saying, as if to no one in particular, but always to her.

He was twice her age. I told him to buzz off, but he ignored me. Finally, I said, "Yes, I wanna dance!"

I then grabbed him and forced him to waltz with me across the floor. I even gave him a peck on the cheek at the end. We did not have trouble with him for the rest of the night.

Despite the apparent joviality of the evening, the children and I were dissatisfied by our first time in a yurt, and longed to spend the night in one—a real one. I had asked Norchayik about yurts, and he had told me that in Kazakh the word for a yurt was the same as it was for a home. So when I asked where we could go to visit a yurt, he replied, "You mean a home? You can come to my home anytime. Anytime is welcome."

"No, not a home like that. I mean a yurt. You know, one like a tent. A *menggubao*," I replied, using the Chinese word for "yurt."

"Oh, one of those. Well you know, I think a regular home is just as good. Why don't you come over to my place?" he answered.

We finally established that while there were some yurts we could rent in the Nanshan (the branch of the Tianshan Range south of where we lived), these were not of the best quality. For a true yurt experience, we would need to go to a place like the Altai or like Sayram Lake.

Try as we might, we could not arrange transport to the Altai

A village of yurts in the shore of Sayram Lake.

from where we lived, so we finally decided to go to Sayram Lake, as it was on the way to Ili, and buses between Shihezi and Ili were cheap and plentiful. Of course, the highway also went through Wusu, so we would at last see where Wusu Beer came from.

As it turned out, there was nothing special about Wusu or the trip out to Sayram Lake. For miles, the scenery as we traveled west towards the Kazakh border was unchanged. On our left were the foothills of the Tianshan Range—the same scene we saw daily from the window of our apartment. On the right was a large gravel wasteland. Periodically, a few ramshackle buildings sprung up from the dust, pretentiously calling themselves a town. Wusu itself had a handful of modest skyscrapers covered with blue mirrored glass, qualifying it as a city rather than simply a town or village.

The new highway to Ili was under construction, but still not open, so for hours, we picked our way slowly along a gravel path running parallel to it. Most of the highway seemed finished, but periodically an unfinished bridge abruptly broke the highway's pavement. Sometimes, one or both lanes of the highway just ended with no warning in a jagged edge overhanging a steep embankment, as though the workers had taken a break and decided that part of the road did not need to be finished.

More often than not, there was wreckage at the bottom of the embankment, evidence that some hapless driver had decided to ignore the warning signs and take the unfinished highway rather than the gravel road beside it.

After hours of constant shaking, the road turned south through a cut between the foothills, and a sparkling blue lake unveiled itself on the right. On the left, in a wide meadow nestled between the forest-covered hills and the road, was a village of thirty or forty yurts. We had arrived.

According to our guidebook, Sayram Lake, at some 6,000 feet above sea level, was "the largest alpine slight alkaline lake in Xinjiang". From that, one could gather that it was big, slightly salty, and in the mountains. "Sayram" is also a place name in Kazakhstan, so it would seem that, even though many of the people living there are Mongol, the name actually has a Kazakh origin. At the same time, the meaning of the name has been forgotten. A similar word in Kazakh means "blessing," so most sources give that as the derivation.

According to one legend, the area of the lake was once just a grassland where a Mongol girl named Qiedan Xue lived. Qiedan fell madly in love with a local horseman named Xuedekeyong. However, a demon became jealous of Xuedekeyong, and wanted Qiedan all for himself. The demon kidnapped her and locked her in his house. For a long time, Qiedan looked for a way to escape, but the demon was always watching her, thwarting her every move. One day, when the demon let his guard down for just a moment, she made a run for it. The demon took up chase and cornered her by a small pool of water. Qiedan dove into the water in the hopes of eluding him. Xuedekeyong saw what was happening and rode to the rescue, killing the demon with his arrows. But it was too late: Qiedan had drowned, and he could not revive her. In his grief, Xuedekeyong jumped into the water, killing himself. The pool of water welled up, as if with his tears, and soon filled the grassland with blue water, forming Sayram Lake.

Emily and William inside a yurt.

Seeing no evidence of demons, but plenty of Mongol lasses and horsemen, we made inquiries, and found an old yurt we could stay in. It was mounted on a wooden platform and had a blue wooden door in the front. Rolled up over the door was a thick piece of felt that could be pulled down at night to help keep out the draft. The peaked dome of the yurt had a hole for ventilation and light. This hole could be covered over with a bit of felt lying on the top of the yurt. Inside, the walls and floor of the yurt were completely covered with plush carpets. A single bare bulb hung from the ribbed ceiling.

While we were at Sayram Lake, we saw a yurt being built. First, a round wooden platform was erected on a level piece of ground. A lattice fence of thin straps of wood was then tied along the rim of the platform. This fence, about the height of a man, would serve as the walls of the yurt. Four curved wooden beams—ribs for the ceiling—were then tied to a round circle of wood, which would serve as the crown atop the domed roof. These ribs and the crown were then raised above the lattice fence, and tied down to it, forming a sort of base. To this base, another forty or so odd ribs were added, all coming to a round peak above the crown. Everything was tied together with rope, and then covered with layers of felt. After these layers were tied down, the whole yurt was wrapped with one large piece of felt. This was held snugly in place by a series of ropes wrapped over and around the yurt.

One thing about it—a yurt is the kind of place where one could comfortably spend a winter where everyday was minus forty degrees outside. The felt provides plenty of insulation, and the construction of the yurt is incredibly airtight. As we were at a fairly high elevation (about 6,800 feet), it was cool during the day and downright chilly at night. The temperatures at Sayram Lake made staying in a yurt tolerable. However, generally speaking, a yurt is not the kind of dwelling one would want to spend a hot (or even a mild) summer in, which brings us to the overall weirdness of some people. While flipping through the TV one night, we saw a story about a husband and wife in California who had decided to build a yurt tree house. From what we gathered by what little English we could hear beneath the Chinese overdubbing, they bought the yurt as a custom-made kit from some mail-order company. They built the yurt on a platform placed in the crook of a tree near their house, and then built a wooden footbridge from the second floor of their house to the yurt. Since yurts are naturally very dark, they put large pictures windows in it so they could look outside, and hung a lamp from the ceiling. Then, since yurts are naturally very hot, they had piped in air conditioning as well. And of course, to make the yurt more comfortable, they had installed a sofa and paneled wooden flooring. Altogether, they were reputed to have spent over $50,000 on this curiosity. The effect was strange to say the least, and raised some troubling questions: When does a yurt cease being a yurt, and become something wholly different and alien? Do yurts exert some strange magical power, like pyramids or dolphins? And, if so, is the power in the shape of the yurt, or the felt, or in something else entirely? Finally, what would our Kazakh friends think of such a yurt?

These are questions with no ready answers. However, after spending days living in a yurt, I do know one thing: Unless there is a blizzard outside or unless you are sleeping, a yurt—a real yurt— is not a place one would want to spend much time in. Yurt-living is nothing more than camping, but with a more substantial tent. The true life of a yurt-dwelling nomad is lived outside. This is life spent outdoors in the sun, the wind, and the dirt. Cooking is done over a campfire. A rock or a mound of dirt substitutes for a chair or sofa. Laundry is seldom done, as without a washing machine the

John inside a yurt.

person doing the laundry may as well take a bath at the same time, and the mountain water is too bitterly cold for that. Yurts have no toilets, making yurt-living very much a back-to-nature kind of experience. In our case, there was a latrine at the edge of the camp. It was a two-story affair with the toilets on the second floor, and a dark pit below. You had to balance on a few slats over the smelly pit, and pray that the shaking building did not collapse while you were squatting.

With yurt-living, the dirt and smells of nature permeate everything, from the tattered clothes you wear, to the hard bed you sleep on, to the smoky food you eat. It is squalid, it is uncomfortable, and it is hard. In short, it is glorious, and we did ever not want to leave.

The Mongols and Kazakhs who stayed at Sayram Lake were mostly shepherds and horsemen, and in the short time we spent there, were able to experience a small bit of their life. Meals were almost entirely made of lamb, which were killed by slitting the throat. This is in order to cause the least amount of suffering, and to drain as much blood as possible from the animal. More than

A Muslim farrier giving a manicure to a horse.

once I saw our future dinner lying on the ground dead with its throat slit. No one thought anything of it. The sheep served as food in the form of meat, cooking fat, milk, yoghurt, and even a hard, salted cheese. They also served as shelter in the form of felt, and clothing in the form of wool. For nomads living a traditional lifestyles, no part of the animal would ever be wasted: Whether it was leather for straps or bones for tools, every part of the animal had use. These were not pets, and there was no sentimentality attached to them. Rather, they were sources of life.

At the same time, the yurt-dwellers seemed more interested in their horses than in the sheep. In many ways, the Mongols and their offshoots have always been people of the horse, and this is shown by the love and care they bestowed upon these animals. Though ostensibly, the horses at the lake were there to give rides to the tourists, the Mongol and Kazakh men and the boys spent most of their time riding or taking care of them. More than once, I would see a couple of boys walking together. One would turn to the other and say something like, "Let's go play!" Then the boys would go running and hop onto the backs of the nearest horses, and ride bareback into the hills, using the manes of the horses for reins.

A Muslim farrier had set up his workshop in the open air on the side of the hill. There, he shod the horses and trimmed their hooves, tying the horses' legs to a thick post in the ground. Apparently, he also served as a kind of vet. There was a small shack off to the side which served as a pharmacy for both people and animals. We bought some cold medicine there, while wondering if

Horses roaming free in the Tianshan Range, with the waters of Sayram Lake in the distance.

the medicine we were given was for a person or a horse.

The horses were at best still half-wild and quite temperamental around strangers when they were roaming free. However, with one of their horsemen on their backs or tugging at their reins, they were completely docile, responsive to even the smallest twitch or movement of their masters. While we were at the lake, they were in the process of breaking one horse. Famously, in the American Wild West, horses were broken by broncobusters, who proved that their will was stronger than the horses' by refusing to be bucked off. Over time, the horses would give in, as breaking a horse involved breaking the horse's spirit. This is not true with the Central Asian riders. Instead of breaking the horse's spirit, they set out to win the horse's trust. They did this gradually. First, they hobbled the horse by tying heavy chains around his front and hind legs. The horse could still move around, but could not walk very well or far. At first, the horse tried to gallop off. However, he was quickly brought to his knees as his legs strained against the chains. Soon the horse just stood there pawing at the ground, trying to break the chains, yet frustrated because he could not.

As we lay in our yurt at night, between the periodic bleating of the sheep, we heard the near-constant rattling of chains, snorting, and hooves pawing on the ground. The horse could find no rest while being chained in this way, and with his racket in the otherwise still night, nor could we. In the morning, the rider would come and whisper soothing words in the horse's ear, and offer him a treat such as an apple. Then he would reach down and loosen the bonds that hobbled the horse's legs. Over a period of time, the back chains would come off, and the front chains would be replaced with loose rope. While the horse was still hobbled, but now gentled, a saddle and reins would be introduced, and the rider would take the horse on short walks, whispering soothing words and giving him treats along the way. Soon, the rider became the horse's only confident and friend, and the horse looked forward to seeing him in the morning because, after all, the rider was the one who loosened the chains and gave him food and comfort. The horse learned that he could not survive without the rider.

Finally, the day would come when the rider would get on the horse's back. The rider would not do this by enforcing his will over the horse. Rather, the rider would accomplish this feat by gaining the horse's permission. In time, the rope binding the horse's legs would come off entirely and the horse would roam free in the pasture, but this would only happen after the horse learned that the rider was his only true companion.

Needless to say, it is a fearful thing for a stranger to ride some of these horses. The horses may have assented to being reined and saddled by a Central Asian horseman, but by what measure can we assume that this assent will also be given to a fat foreigner with a beard? The first horse I tried to ride bucked me off head over heals. Fortunately,

Alpine scenery near Sayram Lake.

John on horseback.

I landed in the soft mud of the hillside and was not too badly injured. We were soon able to find another, much larger horse. Grudgingly and with much complaint, he let me stay in the hard wooden saddle, and we took off. There were seven of us—William, John, Emily, three guides and me. Since William was about three at the time, he rode basically sitting on his guide's lap. The rest of us had our own horses.

We rode far up into the hills, until the lake could no longer be seen. There on the hilltops, we found a grassy meadow where we set the horses to pasture while we lied down and watched the clouds roll behind the snowy mountains in the distance. Everything was so at peace that a guide sat William atop his horse alone. William perched in the saddle grinning and holding the reins, as the horse kept his head down and fed on the greenery. It seemed as though nothing could break the spell. After a while, we got back on our horses and rode over both hill and dale, finally making our way back to the yurts by the lakeside. We were gone, we supposed, for only two hours, and indeed it seemed so short. However, if the clock did not lie, we had really been gone over five. The peacefulness of a mountain meadow can trick you that way.

There are those who think that the highest goal of humanity is to rush forward into development, and rescue people like these, the horsemen of the yurt. After all, their lives are grimy and they do not have many of what we consider the basic necessities of life. Indeed, there is much good in development that many people tend

Emily, William, Debbie, and Samuel pose with local children.

to overlook, and I never met a Kazakh or Mongol father who did not want his son to go to university and get a good job in the city in order to help support his extended family. Having said that, if you asked any of those horsemen where they would rather be, and where they would rather spend their lives, every one of them would have said that they would rather be living in a yurt by some lake or in some mountain meadow, taking care of their horses. Which is why every summer so many of them take up residence in a yurt in some out-of-the-way place. While they may pretend to be in search of some tourist dollar, in truth there is not enough tourism in these places to justify the effort. They are there because this is where their hearts and souls call home. And who can blame them? For despite the inconvenience of yurt-living, we ourselves harbored dark fantasies of throwing it all away, and going to live on a hillside in a yurt, with horses and sheep. Indeed, we sometimes harbor those fantasies even today.

# 9   The Road to Kashgar

Since it was summer vacation, we had the idea that we would go out to visit Mei in her hometown, in Ili not far from Yining, near the border with Kazakhstan. We traveled uneventfully by bus to Yining where we tried to get in touch with her. Somehow, despite many attempts to reach her, our wires got crossed and we were never able to contact her (later, she was quite heartbroken over this). Yining looked like an interesting city, with many of the older buildings sporting signs written in Cyrillic, but it was not a typical tourist destination, and did not have many obvious places to visit or things to do. Consequently, we went shopping for some ethnic goods. I was able to buy a very nice *dombra* (a two-stringed lute, it is the signature musical instrument for the Kazakh people). We went to the bridge over the Ili River and took pictures of ourselves in front of it—a kind of tradition for everyone who comes to visit Yining (sadly, these pictures have been lost). Then we ate at a Uyghur restaurant nearby, and headed back to the hotel.

The next morning, we tried again to reach her. Failing that, we went to the bus station to see where we could go next, and a sleeper bus to Kashgar was available. We were surprised because we did not think that there was a road from Yining to Kashgar. Asking at the counter, we were told that there was now a highway between Yining and Kashgar, and that the trip would only take fourteen hours. Foolishly, we bought the tickets and got on the bus.

As a sleeper bus, there were bunk beds stacked atop one another with about a three-foot space between them. Each level was divided by two aisles running the length of the bus, allowing for rows of narrow berths which were arranged three abreast.

Boys on one side of the road, girls on the other—a bathroom stop in the Taklamakan Desert on the way to Kashgar. There were no real bushes or hills to hide behind, making it hard on the ladies. The bus was a sleeper with bunk beds. No air-conditioning, but everyone had their own window.

The berths could not really be classified as either beds or chairs. Rather, they were cushioned platforms averaging about 4½ to 5 feet in length. These were separated from the berths both fore and aft by metal partitions. A large cushion was provided which could serve alternately as a pillow or a backrest, depending upon whether one wanted to try to lie down or sit up. Fortunately, each berth had its own window, so neither ventilation nor the inevitable bouts of motion sickness would be a problem. As I was by far the largest person on the bus, I got the largest berth, right behind the driver. The rest of our party was studded throughout the bus, which was not as big a problem as we thought it might be, as there was hardly enough room for any of us to sit together anyway, and the noise of the bus's engine and the rushing air was so loud that we could barely hear our own thoughts, much less carry on a conversation.

　　Things went well for the first four hours. The road was fairly clear and smooth and the bus was making good time. Then the bus had a blowout. As it turned out, it also had no spare. The driver left to make a phone call, and soon someone came and put a tire on the bus. However, the tire they put on it was just strong enough to get us to the garage several miles down the road. After several hours at the garage, with the driver and the mechanics sorted old tires, finally deciding which one they wanted to use, patching it, and then putting it on, we took off again. Western China uses Beijing time, so even though it was about 7:30, we had more than three hours of daylight available and the road seemed clear.

As we headed into the mountains, the asphalt turned to gravel. We thought that maybe just this short section was incomplete, that the highway would begin again after a few miles. Then we came to a river and the road just simply disappeared. As the bus turned into the river and began driving through the water, dodging boulders as it went, we came to the gradual realization that there was no highway. Perhaps there would be a highway in the future, and perhaps someday in the future it really would be just a fourteen-hour trip. On the other hand, perhaps not. Maybe the woman at the counter lived in some strange fantasyland of her own, where wishful thinking had its own reality. We simply could not guess.

By this time, it had turned dark, but the bus continued to plow on through the water, sometimes hitting an underwater pothole and almost flipping over. I understand that we missed some beautiful alpine scenery that night, but we were too worried to care.

Finally, sleep overcame our terror. I woke up several times that night. Once, we must have been back on some kind of road. Apparently, we were driving through some military district in the middle of nowhere. We stopped at a guard shack, and a soldier wanted to examine everyone's ID's, so we passed him our passports. The driver then got involved in a long and passionate discussion with the military guard about the presence of foreigners on the bus. It seemed that the guard wanted the driver to turn around and take us back to Yining. Instead, the driver indicated that he would

A hay wagon on the road near Kashgar.

just as soon leave us there at the guard shack and go on. After more discussion and a phone call or two, the guard allowed us through, after first getting the driver to promise that he would not let us get off the bus until Kashgar.

We continued on and I fell asleep. My wife woke up later to hear water rushing as though over a waterfall. The bus began to flip over. Through her window, she could see rushing water looming up to the window. The two substitute drivers and their friends quickly gathered on the opposite side of the bus to counter balance the lean, while the driver turned the wheel and gunned the engine. The bus fell back to earth with a jolt, and she fell back asleep. I woke up again to another guard shack and more discussions, then a gravel road. Hours later, I drifted awake again as the bus hit asphalt. Relieved, the driver said something to his friend. Then, lifting his butt, he let his friend slide beneath him, and they traded places while going 50 mph, without stopping the bus.

We awoke in the morning to find that we had crossed the Tianshan Range and were on the highway from Urumqi to Kashgar. It was smooth sailing for a while, with the mountains to our left and the gravel desert to our right. Around breakfast time, we stopped for a potty break—girls on one side of the bus, boys on the other. There was not so much as a bush to hide behind: just a few piles of gravel here and there. Later in the day, we stopped for lunch somewhere, still many miles away from Kashgar.

Soon after lunch, the highway turned to gravel. As they were in the midst of road construction, the surface of the highway had recently been graded, making it into one long washboard. It was impossible to go more than 20 mph over this surface, and every foot forward caused violent shaking. Just when it seemed that we had reached rock bottom and nothing could get worse, a pregnant Uyghur woman at the back of the bus went into hard labor. Since her berth was too small for her to stretch her legs out in or be attended by anyone, I let her have my place at the front. She sat there moaning at five-minute intervals while another woman wiped her brow. In a panic, the driver tried to go faster, but that just made the shaking worse, and made the poor woman even more miserable. Sometimes her companions would ask the driver how much more time we had left, and the driver would reply that we were not even close. There was no hospital and no clinic out there except in Kashgar, so the driver went for broke and did not stop for dinner. No one wanted him to stop—no one wanted her to have the baby on the bus or on the side of the road.

The hours drug by as we traveled as fast as we could, which is to say, at a snail's pace, until finally past midnight we hit asphalt again on the outskirts of town. The driver mashed the pedal and raced through the streets to the Kashgar bus station. Upon arrival, the pregnant woman was the first off the bus. They rushed her to a cab and took her to the hospital.

The trip had taken 37 hours. We vowed never to take a bus cross-country in Xinjiang again.

# 10 Kashgar

For my family and I, Kashgar will always be one of the most exotic and fascinating places on earth. A city ringed by snowy mountains that sometimes peek out from the distance, it used to be famous for its poplar-lined streets, down which men would drive their donkey carts and woman would walk to the market. However, times have changed. Now it is a city bustling with red taxis, and apartment buildings are springing up everywhere. Despite this, the city is still filled with so much rich culture and history that we never wanted to leave.

A typical street scene in Kashgar. Uyghur men wearing doppas, and women wearing headscarves. A building exemplifying Central Asian aesthetics. Old trucks, freshly slaughtered lamb, and a cart full of watermelon.

## The Old City

The heart of Kashgar, and indeed, of the Uyghur people, is the Old City, which until 1949 was surrounded by a city wall. A small section of this wall can still be found. With urban renewal projects, large parts of the Old City have been torn down since 2001, when I first visited there, but you can still walk down alleyways and get lost, and even forget where you are. You could be in Morocco, Turkey, or Syria for all you knew, if it were not for the occasional street sign in Chinese. Being one of the most strongly

The old beggar asked for tribute for the poor, but I gave him a job as a model instead.

In the Old City of Kashgar, many buildings have a second-floor veranda with ornate trim, where men would sit whiling away the day.

Though I did not notice it at the time, I do not think this Uyghur man enjoyed having his photo taken. The sign behind him is for a dental clinic.

Many of the established shops had pictures showing in explicit—and sometimes gruesome detail—exactly what services they offered.

Muslim urban areas in China, this is one place in China where you might see women wearing burqas, though most women wear colorful scarves and dresses. The Uyghur men can be identified by their blue or grey *doppas* (brimless hats). Typically, these are elaborately decorated with fine needlepoint designs. In tourist areas in Kashgar, sequined red doppas are commonly sold. However, these are for young women and children, and are only worn during festival times.

Though the city is as ancient as time itself, Kashgar had its heyday in the 10th century, and many of the building in the Old City look as though they date from this time. Given the turmoil

Along the streets and alleyways in the Old City of Kashgar.

A pottery shop. The young potters are hiding behind the pots, trying to find some shade.

Blacksmiths beating a red-hot iron. I saw these same men in exactly this same pose in a National Geographic TV special about western China. Since this picture was taken long before *National Geographic* showed up, who is copying whom?

Coppersmiths. From the looks on their faces, we were no doubt just as much a curiosity and a topic of conversation to them, as they were to us.

Along the streets and alleyways in the Old City of Kashgar.

A hardware store.

Some old Uyghur men.

Kashgar has faced over the years, it would be hard to establish if any of the houses really are this old. However, in style and over ambience, the Old City certainly feels like it belongs in the 10<sup>th</sup> century. Nearly all of the houses are made of brick covered with adobe. Some are plastered white. Most are only two or three stories tall, and many of them adjoin, sometimes overhanging the narrow alleyways.

The shops on the main streets are more ornate. Typically, they will have a veranda on the second and third floors, trimmed with a colorful wooden latticework. This serves as a smoking porch for the men, and you can often see them up there, sitting and talking in the shade. Traditional Uyghur shops generally have a sign over the door with pictures of what the shop provides. For example, a tailor might have pictures of pants in various stages of construction, and a dentist might have a picture of a human head with part of the mouth cut away rather grotesquely to show the teeth. The city was full of craftsmen working in trades that were once common in the West, but which are now nearly unknown. Because of the heat, their workshop are usually open, and men often practice their trades in the street. Here you can see blacksmiths, coppersmiths, potters, carpenters, butchers, and bakers, working without electricity and without modern tools, just as their fathers did hundreds of years ago.

A cobbler.

A butcher sharpening his knife, with the carcass of a fatty-tailed sheep hanging behind him.

I am always very uncomfortable taking photographs of people without their permission, so Emily, John, and I hired a guide and translator to help us. It was a good move, as he took us to many parts of the Old City that we otherwise would not have gone to, and it allowed us to speak to the people we saw, none of whom spoke English, and few of whom spoke Chinese.

Despite the drabness of the outside of the houses, many are quite ornate on the inside. Our guide took us to one old house which was open for visitors. The room was paneled in wood painted white. There were several lattice-trimmed alcoves in each wall. These were filled with traditional brass and copper handicrafts. The sunken ceiling was painted in pastel colors, and the floor covered in lush red carpeting. As we sat on cushions around a long table, we were served all kinds of sweet bread, raisins and almonds as we sipped on spiced tea. It was the perfect ending for a long, hot day.

Uyghur children. This was another group that wanted to pose for us when they saw the camera.

Every picture tells a story. Here, a woman calls to her daughter down the street. The girl comes, with her arm held down straight, as if in pique. Where would the girl rather be, if not with her mother?

A woman selling naan. Her smile was as proud as her teeth were gold.

## The Great Bazaar

This is sometimes called the Sunday Market. It is one of the largest and oldest extant traditional Central Asian or Turkish bazaars in the world. With over 5,000 stalls and shops, every kind of daily necessity can be found here, along with all sorts of traditional handcrafts. Bargaining is the rule here.

On my first time at the Great Bazaar, an older Uyghur woman interrupted a transaction between some young salesman and myself. Using her daughter to translate into English, she explained that at even one-fourth the asking price, I was still being cheated. She then went on to publicly scold the salesman, and force him to sell me the product at its usual price, which was less than half what we had agreed on. Since it was a small amount of

The entrance to the Great Bazaar (sometimes called the Sunday Market). This is one of the largest of the old time Turkish-style bazaars in Central Asia.

money, I was embarrassed by her intrusion, and would have been happy to pay what we had earlier agreed upon.

However, it was not about me: It was about the salesman. She was angered by how he was acting. In her opinion, Uyghur people were better than this, and the young man should have known better than to try to cheat someone. In truth, Uyghur people are better than this, and the young man should have known better. In our experience, most Uyghurs will never try to cheat you. However, in the Great Bazaar they will bargain ruthlessly and sometimes get carried away with things like the young salesman did. It is all part of the game in the Great Bazaar—many salesmen there seem to enjoy the bargaining process more than they enjoy getting paid.

Though nearly anything can be bought in the Great Bazaar, tourists are usually most attracted to the silk and wool carpets, fabrics, traditional musical instruments, Uyghur knives, copper ware, and spices.

## Wool and Silk Carpets

These handmade carpets are mostly from Hotan, another oasis city just down the road. When I first visited Kashgar, I met a Pakistani carpet dealer who imported carpets from China into Pakistan, mostly because the price was cheaper and the craftsmanship was high. He explained that apart from Hotan, there were many other towns north of Kashgar which were also good sources of carpets, but was reluctant to name these towns as he was the only international buyer for their carpets and was getting a good deal. The silk carpets were indeed gorgeous. However, even a small prayer carpet could go for over $500 if it was real and of good quality, so we never bought one.

## Fabrics

The most popular choice for Uyghur women is Atlas silk (in truth, much of the Atlas "silk" used for daily wear is synthetic). In other parts of the world, "Atlas silk" refers to the kind of silk

A line of dutar, a two-stringed lute, hanging on the wall of a music shop.

produced by the Atlas moth (*Attacus atlas*), which is the largest moth in the world. These moths are difficult to cultivate, however, so most commercial silk in Xinjiang (and the rest of the world) is produced by common silkworms. To Uyghurs, "Atlas" (or "*etles*" in Uyghur) does not refer to the silk itself, contrary to what some people think ("silk" in Uyghur is "*yipek*"). Rather, "Atlas" refers to the intricate patterns on the fabric. Typically, the patterns alternate four or more bright colors in thin swirls or diamonds that run lengthwise down the fabric. A pleated dress made from this material will inevitably look striped, like a psychedelic tiger. On festival days, many women will were a dress of Atlas silk: Some young women and girls always wear one.

Of course, other fabrics can be found in the Great Bazaar in abundance, especially silks and satins. We could easily buy silk scarves there which would sell for $200 in New York or Tokyo, for less than $10. It was very difficult to get my wife out of the fabric section, and even now she still pines away for it, wishing that she could go back.

### Traditional Uyghur Musical Instruments

The most commonly seen Uyghur musical instrument is the *dutar*, a kind of two-stringed lute. It is like its Kazakh cousin, the *dombra*, but much larger and elaborately decorated with inlaid wood. Most *dutar* are four or more feet in length. A larger *dutar*

Musical instruments, some of them purely decorative, hanging from the ceiling of a music shop.

may be difficult for a person with short arms to play. Since the strings are traditionally made of silk (though common string is used nowadays), it has a softer and warmer sound than most stringed instruments. It can be plucked with a plectrum or strummed with the fingers.

Other instruments include the *dap*, *rawap*, *ghijek*, and *kushtar*. The *dap* is actually a kind of tambourine made of animal skin stretched over a wooden frame. The *rawap* is a kind of lute with from three to six metal strings, some of which are tuned sympathetically to each other, which are played with a plectrum. The slightly oval body can be made completely of wood, or have skin as a soundboard. Above the body, there are ornamental horns that curve down towards it. The *ghijek* is a bowed instrument with a round, bulbous body which sometimes has skin as a soundboard. Below the body, there is a half-moon shaped piece of wood which serves as a leg rest. The *ghijek* is held and played vertically with the leg rest on the player's mid-thigh. Like the *ghijek*, the *kushtar* is a bowed instrument. However, it is all wood and is shaped like a small lute. It is played like the *ghijek*, but has a lower, warmer sound. In addition to these instruments, one can find a variety of horns, stringed instruments, and rattles, some of which defy description, and a handful of Kyrgyz instruments, such as the *khomuz*, can be spotted as well.

An old Muslim graveyard. Since this photo was taken, the graveyard, along with many other old things in Kashgar, has fallen victim to urban renewal. A wide avenue now runs through the middle of it, and all of the graves have been dug up so that the human remains could be reburied elsewhere.

### Yengisar Knives

Uyghur knives are legendary in China for both their sharpness and craftsmanship. It seems that every Uyghur man carries one, and it is said that when a boy is born to a Uyghur family, a knife is placed under his pillow. The best knives are handmade in Yengisar, a small village about forty miles south of Kashgar. The knives are generally made of stainless steel and have elaborately decorated handles. Sometimes the blades have patterns etched in them as well. Typically, the knifes are small, but big enough to serve as basic utility knives or razors (if you dare).

### Copper Ware

One traditional handicraft in Kashgar is copper ware. Pots, pans, and kettles made of pounded red copper are prevalent in the shops. These often have intricate patterns stamped or etched into them. There are also many decorative items made of various copper alloys. Often, these are made of cast metal. The metal is then left outside to oxidize (or treated with chemicals to get the same effect). Afterwards, patterns are etched into it. The bright metal from the etchings contrasts with the dull patina on the surface, making the objects beautiful works of art. Vases, platters, teapots and even animal sculptures, such as deer, are commonly sold.

### Spices

Nearly every spice sold in China can be found in the Great Bazaar, along with a handful of spices which are sold nowhere else.

One specialty of Kashgar were decorative items made of copper and brass alloys. The metal would be cast into the desired shape, and then treated so that a dark patina would develop on the surface. The metal would then be etched, so that the bright metal would shine through.

In particular, various grades of saffron are sold in abundance at only a fraction of what they would be sold for in the West. The Uyghurs generally do not use the saffron for cooking—they use it for a kind of medicinal tea. In conjunction with the saffron, there are various kinds of spiced teas. These generally have a heavy flavor of cinnamon, and are quite refreshing.

Nearby the Great Bazaar, there is a livestock market where you can go to buy sheep, donkeys, horses, and camels. If you do not mind getting muddy, it is worth the trip.

## Id Kah Mosque

In the center of Kashgar, there is the Id Kah Mosque, which is the largest in China. As an outdoor Mosque, most of the central area of the Mosque is actually a large garden with poplar trees and bushes. The few structures of the Mosque include the outer wall, the main entrance, a narrow Main Hall opposite the entrance, a well in the center of the garden, and a few other small buildings along the edges of the garden. Unlike the Emin Khoja Mosque in Turpan, this is a working mosque that regularly holds services. In many ways, it is the main mosque for all of Xinjiang. On a typical day, more than 4,000 people go there for prayer, and on festival days about 30,000 people usually attend prayer either inside the mosque or in the plaza in front of it (one year, over 100,000 people attended a prayer service there).

To underline that this is a place of prayer, the Mosque had a sign at the gate that read,

# Notice to Visitors

The Idkah Mosque is not only a religious place for the Muslims, but also an Important Relic Unit Under the Protection of Xinjiang Uyghur Autonomous Region. So, in order to let the visitors to know how to respect the traditions and customs of the Muslims, we have made the orders as below and hope that you can obey it.

1. All the visitors must buy tickets for entry.

2. If want to use cameras or videocameras, you must buy a ticket for such actions.

3. The visitors who have drunk alcohol and those without proper attire are not permitted for entry.

4. Smoking is forbidden in Mosque.

5. Please Keep the Mosque clean and in good order.

6. Breaking wind and speaking loudly is forbidden.

7. The intimate actions is not welcome in this Mosque.

8. All the visitors must take shoes off before the entry to the Main Hall.

9. The vestors can not enter during the praying time. If some Muslims are praying, you cannot move before them.

10. The assistants of this Mosque have the right to stop unproper actions of the vasitors.

Kashgar Idkah Mosque March 1998.3.18

The prayer hall at the front of the Id Kah Mosque.

The entrance to the Id Kah Mosque. As the largest working mosque in China, in many ways the mosque serves as ground zero for Islam in China. The mosque is an outdoor mosque, which means that apart from the entrance and a very small prayer hall, it is mostly made up of a garden where men gather to pray. On festival days, the plaza in front of the main entrance is filled with men on their prayer rugs.

The site of the Mosque was a graveyard which was built in 996, soon after the area was converted to Islam. In 1442, the local ruler built a small mosque on the site to pray for the souls of his deceased relatives. This smaller mosque was expanded in 1538 to be a worship center for the local population. Since that time, numerous repairs and additions have been made to the Mosque, with most of the current structures dating from the 19th century. The most obvious feature of the Mosque is the main gate. Made of yellow brick and inlaid with multicolor tile, it is a fine example of classic Uyghur architecture.

## Abakh Khoja Mausoleum

On the outskirts of town, there is the Abakh Khoja Mausoleum. For reasons that will be clear later, it is one of the more popular tourist attractions in Xinjiang. It was built as the tomb of Yussup Khoja in 1640. The Khoja branch in Kashgar (the "White Mountain" Khojas) were competitors and distant relatives to the Khojas in Turpan and Yarkand (the "Black Mountain" Khojas). After Yussup Khoja was entered there, the Mausoleum became the family tomb for the White Mountain Khojas, and some 72 members of the clan are buried inside it. The Mausoleum is now named after its most illustrious resident, Abakh Khoja, Yussup's son. Abakh Khoja is regarded by many in Xinjiang as a prophet

Charles, William, Debbie, Samuel and I in front of the Abakh Khoja Mausoleum.

second only to Mohammed in importance. A great missionary for the Muslim faith, he spread his brand of Sufi Islam throughout Xinjiang and even into Gansu and Qinghai, the two adjoining provinces to the east. The Mausoleum is covered in green, yellow, and blue tile, and has an large dome more than 55 feet across. Inside the Mausoleum are the stone sarcophaguses of the family members buried there, each adorned with a satin cover. There is a large graveyard behind the Mausoleum, and various prayer halls nearby. To Muslims, this is one of the most sacred sites in Xinjiang.

The site is popular for many tourists because of the legend of Xiang Fei (the "Fragrant Concubine"), who was reputed to be buried there. For many years, the tomb was known in Chinese as the Xiang Fei Mausoleum, and even today many tourist guidebooks and maps call it that. In Uyghur, Xiang Fei is known as "Iparhan" (the "fragrant girl").

According to legend, Iparhan was one of the most beautiful women in China, and her body had a natural fragrance akin to oleaster. Because of her beauty and her unusual aroma, she was sent to the Qing Emperor, Qianlong, and became one of his concubines. Qianlong was smitten by her, and had a large garden of red date trees planted for her to keep her from getting homesick. In some

A path leading up to the Abakh Khoja Mausoleum. The mausoleum's domed roof is clearly visible in the background.

variations of the story, including some old Chinese operas, Iparhan had a husband back in Kashgar and was not happy in Beijing. Consequently, she tried to kill the Emperor with daggers she had hidden up her sleeve. Failing this, she killed herself. In the most popular legends, however, her relationship with the Emperor was one of the great romances of all time. In one story, the Emperor, out of his love for her, allowed his homesick bride to travel west, but she died of sickness in Inner Mongolia on her way back to Xinjiang. In other stories, she was poisoned on orders from the Empress (or alternately, the Empress Dowager), who was jealous of her and worried about her growing prestige in the court. In the legends, after her death, Emperor Qianlong had a retinue of more than 120 people, led by Iparhan's sister, carry her remains back to Kashgar to bury her in her homeland.

These legends were for the most part creations of the late 19th and early 20th centuries, when the story of Xiang Fei captured the public's imagination and many fanciful ballads, operas, stories and poems were written about her. A poem written by Xiao Xiong in 1892 played a large part in creating the Fragrant Concubine legend. It was only in the early days of the 20th century that the Abakh Khoja Mausoleum became associated with her as her burial place. Since that time, the legends have been kept alive in China by countless books, movies, and more than one popular TV series.

Legends aside, the general consensus today is that the legendary Xiang Fei was a concubine of Qianlong's known to the court as Rong Fei. If she was indeed Rong Fei, her birth name was probably Maimure Aizm, and she was a granddaughter of Abakh

Inside the Abakh Khoja Mausoleum. There are 72 graves here, all belonging to the White Mountain Khoja clan. Despite being associated with the royal concubine Xiang Fei, and even being called the Xiang Fei Mausoleum in many guidebooks and on many maps, Xiang Fie is not buried here, but is buried in the East Tombs of the Qing dynasty in Hebei province. Xiang Fei was probably Maimure Aizm, a granddaughter of Abakh Khoja.

Khoja. As the leading clan in Kashgar, Maimure Aizm's family was captured and taken hostage to Ili by the Junggars in 1715, where she was born in 1735 or 1734. When the Junggars were defeated in 1755, her family was freed from bondage and allied itself with the Qing dynasty to regain control of Kashgar. Soon thereafter, some of the Khojas rebelled against the Qing dynasty. Maimure's clan, however, stayed loyal to the Emperor and helped put down the rebellion. As a reward for this, in 1760, members of the clan were invited to Beijing to be received by the court. They were given residences in the capital, and the male leaders of the clan were granted imperial titles. Maimure was admitted to the ranks of the concubines, which was considered a great honor, and which further helped to consolidate her family's position. Over time, she rose through the ranks to become, in effect, Qianlong's third wife. It is said that he learned some Uyghur from her, and that he allowed her to accompany him on his walks, which demonstrates that she must have indeed been one of his favorites. She died of an illness in 1788, and was buried in the East Tombs of the Qing dynasty in Hebei province. Recent excavations of the tombs reveal that although she was buried in Qing fashion, her tomb had inscriptions from the Koran on it. She never returned to Xinjiang.

When I last visited the Mausoleum, a large sign explained in both English and Chinese that Xiang Fei was not buried there, but was buried in Hebei province. Nevertheless, so strong is the allure of the legend that many Chinese were peeking into the Mausoleum trying to guess which sarcophagus was hers.

# Yusuf Has Hajip Mausoleum

Yusuf Has Hajip (1019?–1085) was born in the city of Balasagun in what is now Kyrgyzstan. Outside of China, he is often referred to as Yusuf Balasagun, as "Has Hajip" is not really part of his name, but just a title. He was a Karakhanid, which was an ethnic group made up in part by the diaspora of the old Uyghur empire, and which later became amalgamated into the modern Uyghur ethnic group. Kashgar was the main city of the Karakhanids, so as an educated and intelligent man, it was natural for Yusuf Has Hajip to go there to live. Over a period of years, wrote a massive poem of more than 6,600 lines called the *Kutadgu Bilig*, which has been variously translated as "The Knowledge Bringing Happiness" or the "Wisdom of Royal Glory." The genre of the poem can best be described as wisdom literature, a genre best exemplified to westerners by the Book of Proverbs. Though written from an Islamic perspective, indeed the *Kutadgu Bilig* often sounds much like Proverbs:

> A man's heart is like a bottomless sea, and wisdom is like the pearl that lies at the bottom.
> If he fails to bring the pearl up out of the sea, it could just as well be a pebble as a pearl.

And,

> The bad are remembered for a curse, and the good for praise. Decide for yourself which one you want. Go then, do good, excellent man, for the deeds of the good always prosper.

After completing the *Kutadgu Bilig* in 1070, Yusuf Has Hajip presented his work to the local ruler, Bugla Khan. The Khan was so impressed that he bestowed upon him the title "Has Hajip," which means "Senior Advisor," and gave him a position in the government.

The *Kutadgu Bilig* has a duel heritage. It was one of the first pieces of literature written in the what is now known as the Uyghur language, and so it is important part of Uyghur culture and heritage. At the same time, Old Turkish is nearly identical to the Uyghur used in the *Kutadgu Bilig*. Indeed, though the pronunciation of Turkish has changed through time, it is said that the languages of Uyghur and Turkish are still close enough that an educated Turk can successfully communicate with an educated Uyghur without the need of a translator. Thus, the *Kutadgu Bilig* is considered one of the most treasured of all Turkish literature by Turkic people everywhere, and Yusuf Has Hajip is featured on the money of Kyrgyzstan.

The Mahmud al-Kashgari Mausoleum, in the countryside west of Kashgar. Mahmud al-Kashgari was a renowned scholar and lexicographer from Kashgar. He compiled the earliest lexicon of the Turkish language, and created one of the earliest maps of the known world.

Yusuf Has Hajip was actually buried in a town near Kashgar. His tomb was enlarged and made into a shrine in the 16th century. However, the tomb fell into disrepair and was threatened by a river, so in 1988 it was reconstructed on its present site in central Kashgar. It is a beautiful building made in the classic Uyghur style, covered with blue and white tiles.

## Mahmud al-Kashgari Mausoleum

Along with Yusuf Has Hajip, Mahmud al-Kashgari (1008–1101) was one of the literary giants of ancient Uyghur literature. Mahmud al-Kashgari was born in Kashgar to locally powerful family from Bargsan, Kyrgyzstan. Though his father was a

The Yusuf Has Hajip Mausoleum. Hajip was the earliest and greatest of Uyghur poets. This mausoleum and shrine was relocated to central Kashgar and reconstructed in 1988. Nevertheless, it is a beautiful example of Uyghur architecture.

The Mahmud al-Kashgari Mausoleum, in the countryside west of Kashgar. Mahmud al-Kashgari was a renowned scholar and lexicographer from Kashgar. He compiled the earliest lexicon of the Turkish language, and created one of the earliest maps of the known world.

Karakhanid, according to some references his mother was Arabic. As his passion in life was linguistics, he traveled throughout Central Asia to research the various Turkic dialects, and to gather information about the people of Central Asia. He compiled this information in his monumental work, *Diwan ul-Lughat al-Turk*, or *Collection of Turkic Words*, completed in Baghdad in 1076. The work is a lexicon of the Turkish language with translations in Arabic. The purpose of the lexicon was to teach the Arab caliphs in Baghdad about Central Asia and its people. For this reason, the lexicon is also a treasure trove of information about the customs and traditions of the people of Central Asia at that time. Though Kashgari's main contribution to history is his lexicographical work, the *Diwan ul-Lughat al-Turk* included a map of Central Asia. One of the oldest extant maps in the world, it is now showcased in a museum in Istanbul, Turkey. On this map, which is labeled in Arabic, Japan in the east is at the top, India in the south is on the left, Iraq and Egypt in the west is on the bottom, and uninhabited Arctic areas in the north are on the left. In the center of the map is

A Uyghur dancer. The groves beneath the Mahmud al-Kashgari Mausoleum are filled with covered platforms where people can sit, drinking tea and eating snacks. Sometimes entertainment is also provided. This dancer kept her hands in front of her face, moving them in a serpentine fashion as she replaced and removed teacups on her head.

Balasagun, with Kashgar over the mountains to its left.

The year of 2008 was declared by UNESCO the year of Mahmud al-Kashgari, in honor of the 1,000 anniversary of his birth, and he is honored throughout Central Asia and in Turkey as the father of Turkic scholarship and learning.

The Kashgari Mausoleum is located about 30 miles west of Kashgar, atop a hill overlooking a graveyard on one side, and a grove of trees on the other. Compared to the other architectural relics in the Kashgar area, it is simple and unadorned. However, this has become an important pilgrimage site for Turkic people. Traditionally, scholars who visit the Mausoleum present their own works there as a tribute of respect to him. Consequently, part of the Mausoleum complex has made a library to store the books left there. The grove beneath the Mausoleum is studded with covered platforms where families can drink tea, have snacks, and even enjoy traditional Uyghur dancing. When we visited, the area was filled to capacity with Uyghurs. From what we could tell, we were the only non-Uyghurs there.

# 11   The Roof of the World

One of my dreams was to travel over the Khunjerab Pass from China into Pakistan. Apart from taking the foolhardy—and illegal for tourists—route from Xinjiang into Tibet (a good way to get killed), or trying to climb K2 (an even better way to get killed), traversing the Karakoram Highway is one of the great adventure treks in Xinjiang. Safer too. The Highway's allure

The Karakoram Highway as it traverses the Pamir Plateau, the roof of the world, at an elevation of more than 10,000 feet.

is based on three things. First, the Karakoram Highway goes up onto the Pamir Plateau, often called the roof of the world. At a typical elevation of greater than 10,000 feet with sections going above 15,000 feet, it is the highest international road in the world. It puts the "high" into "highway." Second, sections of the route are supposed to be among the most scenic in the world. Third, for all of its glamour and fame, it is one of the least visited tourist destinations in China.

The Karakoram Highway follows the old trade route that was part of the Silk Road. For as long as anyone can remember, it has been the only practical southwestern route into China. Consequently, any pilgrim, merchant, archeologist, diplomat, adventurer, or tourist who wanted to go from Persia or the Indian subcontinent directly into China had to take this route. This has been true of nearly all recorded land journeys between these destinations since the time before Christ. Marco Polo traveled through this area, recording that,

> And when you leave this little country, and ride three days north-east, always among mountains, you get to such a height that 'tis said to be the highest place in the world! And when you have got to this height you find a great lake between two mountains, and out of it a fine river running through a plain clothed with the finest pasture in the world; insomuch that a lean beast there will fatten to your heart's content in ten days. There are great numbers of all kinds of wild beasts; among others, wild sheep of great size, whose horns are good six palms in length. From these horns the shepherds make great bowls to eat from, and they use the horns also to enclose folds for their cattle at night. (Messer Marco was told also that the wolves were numerous, and killed many of those wild sheep. Hence quantities of their horns and bones were found, and these were made into great heaps by the way-side, in order to guide travelers when snow was on the ground.) The plain is called Pamier, and you ride across it for twelve days together, finding nothing but a desert without habitations or any green thing, so that travelers are obliged to carry with them whatever they have need of. The region is so lofty and cold that you do not even see any birds flying. And I must notice also that because of this great cold, fire does not burn so brightly, nor give out so much heat as usual, nor does it cook food so effectually.

As we shall see, he gave a fairly good description of the area. Though we saw neither wolves nor sheep there, there is a species of sheep from the Pamir Mountains which exactly fits Polo's description. At present an endangered species, it is called the Marco Polo sheep in his honor.

In Kashgar, we asked around and found that, apart from walking, there was only three ways to get up to the border by way of the Karakoram Highway. One was to ride a bus. There were regular buses between Pakistan and Kashgar that were rather inexpensive. However, technically there were no bus stops or

Mountain vistas as seen from the shores of Karakul Lake. At an altitude near 12,000 feet, Karakul Lake is the highest lake in the Pamir Mountains. It is a mere 10 miles from Tajikistan, 70 miles from Afghanistan, and 110 miles (as the crow flies) from Khunjerab Pass and the Pakistani border. K2 is about 180 miles southeast of Karakul Lake.

layovers once you left Kashgar. Some travelers had been able to purchase tickets all the way into Pakistan, and then convince the driver to let them out before the border. However, they still had to find a way back to Kashgar, and many travelers had found it impossible to get a bus to stop and pick them up for the return trip. Another way was to hitchhike. Some travelers had great luck hitchhiking, but this was not recommended for groups, as most of the vehicles traversing the Karakoram Highway lacked room for more than one extra passenger. The final possibility was to hire a car and a driver. Since we had children and the other possibilities seemed iffy, this is what we chose.

After finding a driver, a man with a van and a border pass, we had to decide how far up the road to go. Going up to the actual border outpost without having a visa to go into Pakistan was out of the question. However, for Americans, visas for Pakistan could only be granted by the Pakistani Embassy in Beijing, so this was not practical. The next possibility was a ride up to Tashkurgan. Tashkurgan is the site of a small Tajik village. Nearby, there are the remains of an old stone fortress which was used to guard the border during the Tang and Qing dynasties. Apparently, it is a fascinating

Mountain vistas as seen from the shores of Karakul Lake. On the far left of this photo, a section of 25,095-high Mount Kongur Tagh. Kongur Tagh is one of the most difficult mountains to climb in the 25,000-foot range, and was not conquered until 1981. Because of the near-constant cloud cover and haze, some of the more distant mountains in this area are usually difficult if not impossible to see.

place. Unfortunately, travel permits to get to Tashkurgan cost over $100 per person, which made it prohibitively expensive for someone on a teacher's salary. They also took several days to get. In addition, Charles was with us, and he had left his ID back in his dorm room, which made it unlikely that he could get past the security checkpoints. The final alternative was Karakul Lake, the lake described in the excerpt from Marco Polo. We still had to get travel permits to go to Karakul Lake, but they were only about $10 each and could be gotten on the same day. Even better, since the security was not quite as tight, Charles would probably be able to come with us. We made the arrangements, and met the driver at our hotel early the next morning.

We made good time for the first hour, until we entered the mountains where we made a rapid ascent. Initially, it seemed a frightful, eerie place. The high peaks were all jagged edges and fresh scree, enveloped in a dry, smoky haze. It was as though the earth had been rent asunder and the ground newly thrust into the sky. Adding to this menacing atmosphere, apart from the cars on the road, the land seemed bereft of any living thing—there were no plants, birds, or animals anywhere to be seen.

The driver himself was worried—not by the road or the mountains, but because of concern about the rapidity of our ascent.

As we were foreigners and our group included young children, his own legal liability would be quite high if anything happened to us. Since one effect of altitude sickness was dehydration, every five minutes, he reminded us to drink water. Not that we needed reminding, as it was exceedingly dry, drier than any desert we had ever visited, and all of our mouths felt full of cotton no matter how much we drank.

"Does any of you have a headache?" he would ask. After having all the moisture sucked out of our sinuses, of course we did.

Every time one of the kids moved, he would shout out, "Is he going to throw up?" An absurd question, since he was driving like a maniac over mountainous roads full of switchbacks. It was a miracle that none of us threw up. Yet, he made it clear that at the smallest excuse, he would turn back, because he did not want the responsibility of anyone getting sick or dying. Therefore, we said nothing.

Lest one thinks that we were taking our lives in our hands, some perspective is needed. When I was a child, I often used to visit my grandfather in Denver, and he would take me driving up in the Rocky Mountains at elevations high or nearly as high as the road we were on. I do not recall getting sick or dying because of it. Nor have I heard cases of many people getting sick or dying of altitude sickness because they went skiing in Vail (at an elevation of 8,000 feet) or climbed one of Colorado's many 15,000-foot peaks. I am sure it happens. However, I am also sure that we were more likely to have gotten killed in a car accident because the driver was not watching the road while speeding around hairpin curves.

In frustration, we pled for him to slow down, but he was too obsessed with whether or not we were suffering from a headache to pay any mind to our pleas. He kept telling us how dangerous the trip was, but the only danger we felt was from him.

Finally, we reached a military checkpoint, a lonely shack beside a roadblock, and we had to stop. Since the driver had a border pass, they let him drive through. Meanwhile, we each had to

A rest stop on the Karakoram Highway. This particular section is paved.

walk one by one down a narrow corridor running down the side of the shack, where we were questioned, and then let through. Charles got the worst of it, simply because he had forgotten his ID. Fortunately, he looked like exactly what he was—a young college student naive enough to think that on a trip across country his ID was safer and more useful in a drawer back in his dorm room, rather than in his pocket. After a stern warning to the driver that Charles better be in the van on the return journey, they let us through.

Shortly after the checkpoint, the highway turned to gravel in many places. As the driver explained, every winter avalanches of ice and snow would cause the road to crumble, then the runoff from the spring thaw would finish the job, washing the road away. Just as surely as this would happen, bulldozers would come to plow the road open again, and they would begin to repave it, finishing just before the first snow, when the process would begin again.

Thankfully, because of the road conditions we had to slow down. In some parts, only one lane of gravel was available. Traffic jams would develop, as cars took turns navigating the road, hugging the boulders on one side, while trying to stay away from the soft shoulder of gravel overlooking the cliff on the other side.

The worst traffic jam kept us waiting in line for over an hour. There had apparently been a bridge that had crossed over what— in the spring—had been a rushing river that cascaded down the mountainside in a waterfall. However, this year the river had washed the bridge away. Now the river was nothing more than a stream rushing around islands of gravel and boulders before falling headlong over a cliff. There was only one path through the maze of

The Karakoram Highway. Here, the road has been totally washed out by the raging waters of the spring thaw. In front of us, a field of boulders and a rushing stream. To the right, a sheer drop and a waterfall. To the left, a high mountain. There was only one practical route through the boulders, so vehicles had to cross one at a time. Eighteen-wheelers, buses, four-wheel drives, vans, and even a mini-car or two were backed up for miles on either side of the washed-out road.

boulders, so we sat waiting as eighteen-wheelers, buses, vans, four-wheel drives, and even mini-cars slowly picked their way through. A backhoe sat nearby, waiting to pull vehicles out in case they got stuck.

Despite road conditions, the traffic was heavy. After the traffic jam, I saw a bus from Pakistan bearing down on a thirty-degree incline, leaving a trail of dust behind it. It was so crowded with people that even the middle aisle was full. Sitting in the middle on the front row, with no seatbelt and with his face no more than a few feet from the unobstructed windshield, there was a foreigner wearing a T-shirt and carrying a backpack. I wondered, was he simply the last person on the bus? Or, did he actually choose this seat because he wanted a good view? I have no idea which. However, his face was as white as a sheet and he had a look of sheer terror mixed with nausea. It made me wonder what lie on the road ahead.

As it turned out, soon after we saw the bus, the road leveled out and became pavement again. The backpacker must have been looking at the road ahead, rather than thinking about the road he had just passed through. We were now on the Pamir Plateau. On

Mountain vistas as seen from the shores of Karakul Lake. At an altitude near 12,000 feet, Karakul Lake is the highest lake in the Pamir Mountains. It is a mere 10 miles from Tajikistan, 70 miles from Afghanistan, and 110 miles (as the crow flies) from Khunjerab Pass and the Pakistani border. K2 is about 180 miles southeast of Karakul Lake.

The picture I could not leave Xinjiang without taking—a herd of yaks grazing on the Pamir Plateau.

either side of the road stood tall mountains—some had snowcaps, others were covered in white sand. Beside the road, there was a small steam with grass growing on its banks. Periodically, we saw herds of goats and yaks grazing there. Most had collars on them, signifying that they had owners. However, we saw no houses or people.

After about an hour, we rounded a bend and came to a pristine blue lake sitting at the base of a high mountain. We had arrived. At an elevation of about 12,000 feet, this was Karakul Lake. The mountain was the 24,757-foot Muztagh Ata.

Near the edge of the lake, there was a small hut and a handful of old, grey yurts. Down the road, sat a small hotel and dining hall for truckers. Our driver dropped us off at the yurts and drove off to the hotel, promising to pick us up later. We were glad to be rid of him.

After inquiring at the hut, which as it turned out served as a

We saw a number of camels roaming free in Xinjiang, and this was one of them. Since wild camels supposedly no longer exist in China, perhaps his owner was nearby.

kind of Kyrgyz restaurant, we rented a yurt and stashed our gear. Then we each took off in separate directions to explore the area. Apart from some camels, a few horses, and their handlers, the place was completely desolate. There could not have been more than twenty people on the banks of the lake, the hotel and guests included.

Finally, I thought, a chance to be alone and enjoy nature. I went walking to the farthest end of the lake, where I sat down. Sure enough, after I had been sitting there for five minutes, a man appeared over the far hills on the horizon. Suspiciously, I wondered if he was walking my direction. After fifteen minutes, it was obvious that he was coming to meet me: There was nothing behind me that he could be walking to. He continued for some time, before finally drawing near. I braced myself for the encounter, thinking he might be a bandit or someone else up to no good.

"Hi! Bob!" He exclaimed cheerfully. "It's been such a long

time since I've seen you. What? Hasn't it been two or three years?"

"I've never seen you before," I replied.

"Of course, you have!" He answered. "You're Bob! That Hindi man. You've been here several times! Don't you remember me?"

"No. My name is not Bob and I have never been here before."

Perplexed, he peered closely at my face. "Are you sure that you aren't Bob from three years ago?"

"Yes, I'm sure I'm not Bob."

He stood back, and puzzled over things for a moment. Then he said, with a loud grin, "Well, then. Would you like to buy a watch?" He opened up his coat, and sure enough, there were about twenty watches pinned inside it.

I do not know whether to laugh or cry. This was the last place in the world I wanted or expected to be accosted by a street vendor.

Of course, our conversation was in a combination of pigeon Chinese and English. Apart that, everything happened just as reported. Events like this are too strange to make up.

Apart from looking at the scenery, skipping rocks, and avoiding salesmen, there was not much to do. We ended up

Mount Muztagh Ata.

Camels on the shores of Karakul Lake.

spending a lot of time going to the Kyrgyz restaurant. It was a squalid affair, with no windows and a single bare light bulb that barely pierced the darkness. Apart from food, the owner sold Kyrgyz felt hats and other ethnic gear. I think we bought nearly everything he had.

The food itself was greasy and unmemorable, except for the yak yoghurt. It had a slight off-taste that we usually associated with the lamb butter or Kazakh cheese we sometimes got, but otherwise tasted quite good. As rich and creamy as anything I had ever eaten before, I thought it was exquisite, and could not eat enough of it. A European couple came into the hut once and asked what was good, so I recommended it to them. They eagerly bought a few cups of the yoghurt, and took a big spoonful before spitting it out and rinsing their mouths with some warm tea. This puzzled me. Perhaps their taste buds were more refined than my own. Or, perhaps I had lived in Xinjiang for too long.

At night, after the children were asleep in the yurt, my wife and I went out and sat by the lake. Though the daytime had been quite mild, it was now cold and we had trouble keeping from shivering. The night was moonless, and there were no lights to

John skipping rocks on Karakul Lake, against the backdrop of Mount Muztagh Ata. At 24,757 feet, Muztagh Ata is one of the more prominent mountains on the Karakoram Highway. Unlike Kongur Tagh, it is considered one of the easiest mountains to climb in its height class.

be seen anywhere in the valley. Looking up at the sky, the stars shimmered so brightly as to almost cast a shadow. In the starlight alone, we could clearly see the lake and the mountains around us. Each star seemed magnified, like a small jewel in the sky. So bright were the stars and so clear was the night, that we could easily see all the stars' individual colors of different shades of red, orange, and yellow. Many nebulas were also clearly visible, like small oceans of deep-blue clouds nestled in the blackness. I tried to pick out the different constellations, but there were so many stars shining so brightly that it was impossible to do so. The Milky Way looked milky, like a cloud, with hundred of thousands of multicolored diamonds imbedded in it. We wondered if this was what the sky looked like to astronauts floating in space. In this desolate place, we felt like two people all alone, sitting on the roof of the world. In a weird way, this must be how astronauts feel while orbiting the earth.

We could not stay out because of the cold and because we did not bring coats. However, the brightness of the starlit sky stayed with us long after we returned to our dark yurt, and is even with us today.

# 12 Saying Goodbye

All good things must come to an end, and so it was with our time in Xinjiang. Ultimately, we had to leave because of our children. If the choice had been mine alone, I would probably still be living in Xinjiang. I had all the time in the world, my job had comparatively little stress, and I loved the natural surroundings, the people, and the peace I enjoyed there. However, the area was too remote, too distant from the rest of China, not to mention the rest of the world, to be a viable place to bring up a foreign family. Our kids had no educational opportunities, no English books, and no chance of experiencing their own culture. It is true that they had a rich, and welcome opportunity to find out about different cultures. However, after two years, there were fewer places in Xinjiang for them to explore and fewer things for them to discover. The negatives began to outweigh the positives. For their sakes, we had to leave.

I put the word out, and eventually found a new job in eastern China. So, in late July, after the final exams were finished and I had posted my students' grades, we had a last going away party with Norchayik and his family, and then another with the Pakistanis. We packed our things, and had them shipped by train to our new home. Then, we went to the Shihezi train station for a final journey out of Xinjiang. Mei, Charles and a handful of other people saw us off at the station. A day later, the train was taking us through the Hexi Corridor in Gansu province, and we were no longer in Xinjiang.

It is now several years later. Mei, our Hui friend, has fulfilled her dream, and is working in Shanghai for a foreign company. Aliya, our former maid has opened a clothing store in Urumqi.

Emily poses in front of karakul lake.

As she was always quite fashionable in her Uyghur way, this is something which well suits her. Charles, my former student from Hami, impressed everyone so much with his English skills that he is now a teacher at Shihezi University, while Norchayik is a salesman based in Urumqi, with accounts in Pakistan and Kazakhstan. We like to think that we inspired and helped each of them to attain their dreams, but, in truth, whatever life they have is a credit to their own aspirations and hard work, and not to our own.

As for us, Emily is now an aspiring actress and model. She has had some success in this, having been in TV commercials and films with some very famous Chinese stars. However, she has yet to hit the big time—in each of the productions she has been in, if you blink, you miss her. After all of these years, John has finally left his bedroom, and, to our pleasant surprise, can play the guitar well enough to find work doing it. Samuel and William are still very young. They barely remember the time we spent in Xinjiang.

Though my wife and I have not returned to Xinjiang, Emily and John have both been back—Emily several times. As is often said, you can't go home again, and so although Xinjiang is in many ways in their hearts as home, their return was bittersweet. Like much of China, Xinjiang has changed greatly in even the short time since we left. Many of the things they so nostalgically remembered no longer exist as they once were. Other things which they so eagerly wished to experience again did not seem as good as before. In their minds, nearly all of this change is for the worse. And indeed, some of it is for the worse. There is a great appeal in the old neighborhoods, the old ways, the ancient way of life. Some simple things, like being able to ride into the wilderness on horseback, are better than their modern replacements. Indeed, some simple things of the past have no modern equivalents. Yet, at the same time, people have to live and to eat. Despite the romantic appeal of the past way of life, the people of Xinjiang have aspirations and deep needs that must be attended to. Like old age, progress and change must come, whether one wants it or not. Thus, with both sadness and with hope for the future, Emily and John were forced to witness the passing away of some things that were cherished, and some things which cannot be replaced.

At the same time, we all look back with amazement. Was there ever a time such as this, when we rode camels up mountains of sand? When we traveled through deserts and mountain passes most people only know of through legend? When we stayed in yurts, drinking salted mare's milk and eating roasted lamb? As I sit in a modern office typing on a computer, it all seems like an impossible dream, like it could not have ever happened. Yet, it is all true.

# Bibliography

——. *Guide to Xinjiang*. Hong Kong: Hong Kong China Tourism Press, 2001.

——. "Legend of Xiang Fei." *Kashgar, Xinjiang, China*. http://www.kashi.gov.cn/english/Context/History07.htm.

Bai, Leslie. "Road Xinjiang Bole Sarim Lake (Xailimuhu) (Yongfei Gu)." *I write, I blog,* May 4, 2008. http://lesliebai.blogspot.com/2008_05_01_archive.html.

Brewster, Colin and Muhammed Tursum Abullah. *Travelling in Xinjiang: A Uyghur Conversation Guide for Tourists*. Urumqi, China: Xinjiang People's Publishing Press, 1997.

Ding, Xiaolin, ed. *The Ruins of Ancient Gaochang City*. Liu Linqian, trans. Urumqi, China: Xinjiang Art Photography Press, 2001.

Faxian. *A Record of Buddhistic Kingdoms*. James Legge, trans. Oxford: The Clarendon Press, 1886.

Hajip, Yusuf Has. *Wisdom of Royal Glory (Kutadgu Bilig) A Turco-Islamic Mirror for Princes*. Robert Dankoff, trans. Chicago and London: The University Of Chicago Press, 1983.

Li, Kai. *Kashgar—Xinjiang, China*. Urumqi, China: Xinjiang People's Publishing Press, 1989.

Lou, Wanghao. *The Grand Sight of Xinjiang's Folk-Customs*. Liu Linqian, trans. Urumqi, China: Xinjiang Art Photography Press, 2001.

Polo, Marco and Rustichello of Pisa. *The Travels of Marco Polo*. Henry Yule, trans. London: John Murray, 1875.

Shi, Xiaoqi. *Entering Xinjiang*. Tsui Yenhu and Wang Fengxia, trans. Urumqi, China: Xinjiang Art Photography Press, 2006.

Urumqi Zhongqing Culture Media, Ltd. *The Ten Major Enigmas in Xinjiang*. Urumqi, China: Xinjiang Art Photography Press, 2001.

Wu, Cheng'en. *Journey to the West*. W.J.F. Jenner, trans. Beijing: Foreign Language Press, 1955.